BOYS WILL PUT YOU ON A PEDESTAL

(so they can look up your skirt)

A DAD'S ADVICE FOR DAUGHTERS

PHILIP VAN MUNCHING

with a Foreword by Katie Couric

SIMON & SCHUSTER PAPERBACKS

New York   London   Toronto   Sydney

SIMON & SCHUSTER PAPERBACKS
Rockefeller Center
1230 Avenue of the Americas
New York, NY 10020

First Simon & Schuster paperback edition 2005

SIMON & SCHUSTER PAPERBACKS and colophon
are registered trademarks of Simon & Schuster, Inc.

For information regarding special discounts for bulk purchases,
please contact Simon & Schuster Special Sales at
1-800-456-6798 or business@simonandschuster.com

Designed by Jeanette Olender

Manufactured in the United States of America

1   3   5   7   9   10   8   6   4   2

Library of Congress Cataloging-in-Publication
Data Control Number: 2005042454

ISBN 0-7432-6778-8

ACKNOWLEDGMENTS

The author would like to thank:

Connie and John Sargent for taking an interest,

Geoffrey Kloske for taking a chance,

Katie Couric for so generously offering when I was too polite to ask,

Catherine Bradford, Nellie Sciutto, Mary Solomon, and Brett Thomasson, for their insightful (and gently given) comments on the manuscript,

Dave Spalthoff for giving me a place to write,

Christina Barbara Fiore Van Munching, my love, for just about everything,

Steve Martin, whose joke inspired the title,

and

Elizabeth Auran, my doppelgänger, part-time editrix, and the person most responsible for the book you now hold in your hands.

CONTENTS

FOREWORD

A NOTE TO PARENTS FROM KATIE COURIC

Almost everyone with children agrees that being a parent is one of the hardest jobs in the world. It's also one of the most important: as Jacqueline Kennedy Onassis said, "If you bungle raising your children, I don't think whatever else you do well matters very much." Guiding our children, helping them to grow up with solid values, healthy self-esteem and a desire to contribute to society are the goals . . . but our self-imposed report cards are impossible to calculate as we go along, except the A for effort. Our final PGPA (parenting grade point average) will only become clear when our children are well on their way.

The parenting sections at chain bookstores take up a daunting number of shelves. We are constantly inundated with advice in books, magazines, on television, and from our friends and relatives. At the same time, we parents are assaulted by forces outside our control. Images in popular culture seem to make a hard job even harder. Raising kids today means grappling with the perils of the Internet, the over-sexualization of just about everything, the complexities of the world around us, and the feeling, since September 11th, that we are no longer as safe and secure as we once were. Our job as parents may be more difficult than ever . . . but clearly, against this backdrop, it's never been more important.

It doesn't take a rocket scientist to know that communication is key. Talking to our kids about the important stuff—like death, faith, sex, and friendship—is something we all mean to do more of. And yet somehow, we can't always manage it. We wonder if our timing is right, we worry we'll say the wrong things . . . and sometimes we're just plain scared to face these frankly scary topics ourselves. That's where my personal Dr. Phil comes in.

I first met Philip Van Munching when we exchanged jokes at an event at our daughters' pre-school. I liked him immediately; he is funny, kind, wise, culturally aware, skeptical when skepticism is required, and sentimental when a moment calls for sentimentality. Caring and compassionate, he is always willing to listen. Philip has become one of my closest friends and confidantes, and his advice is sage, sweet, droll, and right on the money.

It's the way he dispenses that advice that makes this book, well, indispensable. In the pages that follow, Philip talks to daughters without ever talking down to them. He shows that parental guidance doesn't have to come in a series of lectures, it can be given in loving, supportive (and funny) conversation. And whether his subject matter is the best way to deal with a broken heart, how to find faith, or even why it's a really, really bad idea to get a tattoo, he manages to be a nimble storyteller and a wise guide for young women.

Most important, Philip is an überdad. He loves his two girls and would like nothing better than "good father" to be the headline of his obituary. In writing this beautiful, funny love letter to his darling daughters, Anna and Maggie, Philip has given each of us a valuable blueprint for broaching some of life's touchy issues with our own children.

INTRODUCTION

IF I STEPPED IN
FRONT OF A BUS

I'm not entirely sure whether it's a sign of pragmatism or just an advanced stage of whistling in the dark, but as I get older I seem to be having a lot more conversations that begin with this: "If I died tomorrow . . ." Actually, that's not quite right. Other people put it that way. I like to be more folksy. I always say, "If I stepped in front of a bus tomorrow . . ."

Which almost turned into a prophecy on a warm afternoon some months back, when I very nearly did just that. I damn near stepped in front of a bus.

It wasn't the bus that almost killed me, at least not at first. It was the panel truck that the bus blocked from my view. I stepped off the curb of Fifth Avenue and Thirty-third Street, certain that I could cross against the light; certain that I'd gauged the speed of the M3 bus correctly and, with just a slight jog, I would be on my way to the subway that much faster. Somewhere between being right in front of the driver and having cleared the bus entirely, I realized my mistake—and I stepped backward as the truck blew

1

past me. I stepped backward into the path of the bus. There was a horn; I can't tell you whether it was the truck's or the bus's, or whether it was just the noise adrenaline makes when it's being pumped to one's every extremity at once, because I remember only the sound. And I remember the sound only because it somehow wove itself into the intense and immediate sense of panic I felt. I don't even recall looking at the bus driver or how my legs got me back to the west side of Fifth Avenue. I know only that the bus kept going, missing me by a very little bit, and I got back to where I started.

Here's an interesting medical theory: If the heart races to five trillion beats per minute, short-term memory ceases to function. Maybe it's a problem of blood flow.

However I avoided becoming a part of New York City's asphalt, the important part of the story is not that I was lucky (and how!) nor that I was incredibly stupid (guilty as charged, Your Honor), but rather that my goose was very nearly cooked. This was suddenly for me not some lofty conversation about how I would like to be remembered, this was "*Ohmygod* I nearly widowed my wife and left my children fatherless." This was also the first time I could ever recall feeling the need to do a little inventory on that part of the soul where regrets are stored.

And you know what? I couldn't find any. While there were plenty of things I felt bad about, and even more that still make me flush with embarrassment, there was nothing that had any urgency to it. Nothing that I hadn't done that would've caused me to lose sleep; no serious trespass against anyone that I hadn't asked forgiveness for.

For a guy who'd just stepped in front of a bus, I felt pretty good. Except for one nagging thought. Call it a pre-regret, if you'd like. If I had stepped off the curb in front of that bus and died stupidly and tragically—or even if I had died heroically, pulling children (and nuns and puppies) from a sinking boat in the East River—my last thought would have been this: I haven't shared with my daughters all the things I meant to as they grow up, like telling them all of the experiences I've had that might actually be of some use to them as they make their way in life. I would have regretted not passing along to them the lessons that I've learned from the mistakes I've made, the things I've gotten right, and the good advice that I've been given.

That night, after squeezing my wife and daughters just a little tighter than usual, I lay awake wondering if there was a way to avoid that regret. Maybe for the first time since becoming a dad, I thought about how I would talk to my girls about the really important stuff, and when. Should I wait until things come up in their lives, and try to comment on them as they happen? Should I hold my tongue until I'm asked? Should I be reading 548-page books by guys with degrees in child psychology and taking notes? What if my daughters won't listen to me? What if they think I'm too pushy/annoying/dumb/out-of-touch? *What if I give lousy advice?* Needless to say, sleep did not come easily.

Over the next few days, I thought a lot about the best advice I've gotten, and where it came from. I realized pretty quickly that the stuff that's helped me most in life came from all kinds of different sources, but always in the same way. Supportively. *Conversationally.* I don't think I've followed a single piece of guidance that was given to me by someone who was lecturing; nothing that started with "Let me tell you something" or "You need to listen to this" has ever sunk in very deep. All the good stuff has come in conversation, usually with people who were simply passing along their own experiences.

Suddenly parenting didn't seem quite so daunting. Maybe I didn't need to have a series of lectures prepared—they'd likely fall on deaf ears, anyway—but instead I could focus on explaining to my girls how I had come upon my own beliefs. I needed to be able to tell them not only *what* I'd learned but also *how* I'd learned it.

Of course, that still left the problem of the bus. On the chance (hopefully slim!) that the Grim Reaper should decide to visit me anytime soon, I figured it would be best if I wrote down the things I most wanted my daughters, Anna and Maggie, to know. About the same time that I started seriously thinking about what I hoped would eventually be a bunch of letters to my girls, I found myself writing letters to my friends' daughters, to mark big events in their lives, both good and bad. It was my grateful friends, telling me later that those notes served as good conversation starters with their girls, who gave me the idea for this book.

It occurs to me that there's a benefit to passing experience on by writing it down, and that's *distance*. Most advice, most life guidance, is given in some context. It's given at the moment it applies, which means that it's often tainted by the particulars of that moment, for example:

If the day comes that either of my girls comes home from high school with a forty-year-old boyfriend, I sincerely doubt the twin Furies of fear-for-her and rage-at-him will allow me to give a reasoned argument as to why he's not a great choice. (Even if I could, I suspect the homicidal way I'd be looking at him would make listening to me pretty hard.)

Writing it all out removes the limitations brought on by context; limitations not just on a dad's ability to give counsel, but also on a daughter's ability to hear it. My wife and I are learning—slowly, but we're learning—not to let discussions of important things go on too long if one or both of us are angry . . . especially at each other. Angry minds are seldom open, and I would guess scared or miserable minds function the same way. That is, they *don't* function. Distance, whether it's achieved by walking around the block to cool off or spending the time to put what you feel on paper, is the most important tool you'll have in dealing with situations in your life. Distance dampens anger and calms fear; it'll serve you well, if you let it.

Consider all that follows on these pages as a father's advice, given as he would most like you to hear it; guidance that's from the heart and the mind and *not* from the reactive gut. These are life lessons that are passed along with a sense of hope, not a sense of urgency or resignation. This is guidance that comes with a healthy dose of distance.

But understand that the word "distance" refers only to the removal I feel, as I write this, to the specifics of the questions a daughter might ask and the situations that she may be in as she grows up. There isn't the slightest bit of distance in the feelings that I have for my girls as their father. The chapters ahead are a distillation of what I know about the world, which I hope you'll use as you see fit. First, though, let me tell you what I know about being a dad:

Daughters are dreams come true. For me, that's literal: it was always my dream to be the father of girls, just as some men dream of playing center field and others dream of running large companies. I wanted daughters. It'd be swell to be able to explain why to you, but I can't. Whatever the reason, getting what I wanted has proved humbling, in that it has revealed the inadequacy of my imagination—I never in my wildest dreams imagined the depth of emotion being a dad has brought out in me.

I realize the sappiness of writing that last bit . . . but I revel in it. And perhaps that's the greatest gift a daughter can give her father. Because they haven't yet amassed a lifetime of hang-ups or gender notions (or any of that fun stuff that cost my fellow New Yorkers two-hundred dollars a forty-five-minute hour to hash out with professionals), my girls have helped me see what's missing from a life led with emotional caution. They've taught me that there's no shame in the tears that form when one of them tells me, solemnly, that they love me "bigger than the moon and stars," and that there's plenty of shame in not recognizing such moments as the best that life could ever offer. Having daughters has taught me that the words "I love you" shouldn't be saved for private moments, but should be shouted across Grand Central Station at the height of rush hour. The good stuff—love, happiness, and pride—needs to be celebrated openly and regularly. I plan on spending the rest of my life thanking my girls for teaching me that.

One other thought before we start, a quick note on what I guess I'll call "Dead Bird Syndrome."

Some time ago, I was walking my younger daughter, Maggie, to the garage where we park our car. She was singing that god-awful "Titanic" song for the millionth time to me while I was remarking upon how grown up she seemed now that I no longer had to carry her. (My knees and my back were particularly thankful.) We were both smiling and chattering away . . . until I saw a dead bird in our path. So I did what parents do: I distracted her until we were safely past the brown shape on the sidewalk. And she did what children do: she laughed when I scooped her up and swung her around, and she remained wonderfully oblivious to my reason for doing so.

7

It was only later that I realized I'd done Maggie a disservice. My intentions were good, but in shielding her from evidence of a very basic fact of life, I robbed her of the ability to notice it and to talk about it and maybe to put it in its proper place. I'm not melodramatic enough to think that the one instance has any great significance—like it would cure her of the fear of death, or anything—but I do believe that my impulse was wrong in that case. It's the little, everyday examples of tough things like death that help prepare you for the big, infrequent examples.

So, I'll continue to hustle her out of the room when the evening news wallows in the latest mindless act of cruelty, but I'll try a bit harder to stop acting like a human blinder. I'll try a bit harder to let her see the *whole* world, and the flaws included therein.

That includes *my* flaws, many of which are detailed on the pages that follow. I hope that it won't embarrass you, kind reader, to know some of the silly and stupid things I've done over the past forty-two years. Please also know that it doesn't embarrass me to tell you about them. Like that dead bird on the sidewalk, most parents think their own blunders are unpleasant realities best hidden and forgotten. But I've learned a little something about mistakes: They are the truest measures of you, both in what prompted you to make them, and what (or whether) you choose to learn from them. They are what define you and what teach you. And they are maybe the only things in your life that are truly your own. Everyone will jump in to

8

grab a little glory when you do something right; mistakes are yours and yours alone. The trick is in how you make use of them.

That's confusing, I know. Let's try it this way:

My older daughter Anna and I once built a fort out of cushions and blankets and towels and chairs. It was incredibly elaborate, as those things go; we even brought a battery-powered lamp into it, to read *Yertle the Turtle* by. It took us about half an hour to get it right. About ten minutes into making it, she wanted her Barbies to sit along one stretch of blanket by the coffee table and started piling them on. The whole thing collapsed. Anna pouted for a minute, then said, "Wait, I know let's do." (It's remarkable how much I miss the garbled syntax of her four-year-old self.) She got a box from the dining room, set it up on the coffee table, and draped a blanket over that. Just about each and every Barbie fit on that contraption.

And when her grandmother came over, that was the only part of the fort Anna wanted to show her. Her silly father was crowing about the door flaps and the reading room, and about how the American flag blanket was draped *just so* over the side of the dining room chairs, and Anna made sure her Nana saw how a strategically placed box could hold the weight of a dozen dolls. Because she'd made a mistake and because fixing it took some thought and effort, that part of our fort was the one that she was proudest of.

Most folks think that mistakes get bigger and more important than that as they get older, but they don't, mostly. Except for the major errors that destroy lives, most mistakes are about as consequential as the temporary collapse of that fort. The only difference is that as you grow up you find your mistakes more embarrassing . . . the world has a way of convincing you that if you goof something up, you're somehow diminished. That to admit failure, no matter how small or correctable, is a weakness. That's just completely absurd. If you're willing to learn, each false start is more experience to help you trust the path you eventually find. Each mistake is a chance to show yourself that the things worth achieving are worth the effort of trying again and again.

So here's my first piece of advice to you, and maybe the most important one between these covers: Make glorious mistakes. If you can, try *not* to make them out of laziness or meanness. Make them instead because you are over-reaching your abilities. Make them because you bit off a bit more than you can chew. Make them because they will prove to the world—and more important to yourself—that you are striving, and not coasting. Don't be too self-critical; no one who really loves you expects you to be perfect. Count on failing every so often, so when success comes, you'll know you've earned it.

Oh, and listen to your old man, from time to time.

CHAPTER ONE

STUFF

My friend Dave sold stereos to make money for college. He told me that his typical customer fell into one of three categories: people who wanted to buy the best quality, people who wanted to pay as little as possible, and people who couldn't care less about quality or price. This last group was after something he called *flash*.

Since the job could be really boring, Dave and the other salesmen came up with ways to entertain themselves, mostly by goofing on the customers. One of the things they liked to do best was mess with the guys who came in and pretended to know everything about stereo equipment. These guys often fell into the "flash" category.

Here's how it worked: If Dave thought some customer was acting like a know-it-all, he'd immediately take the guy—it was always a guy; girls don't mind admitting that a salesman may know more about what he's selling than they do—and would show him the most expensive stereos. Then Dave would pepper him with technical language, most of it made up. "The bass response from this model has

11

passed the Chester standards, tweaking in five pulse units at the lower frequencies," he'd say. (Though, as far as he knew, there's no such thing as a "pulse unit," and there are no Chester standards. Chester was his friend's mutt of a dog.)

Now, if the guy stopped Dave and asked him to explain, he'd bring him back to the well-priced, nonflashy stuff and do his best to give the guy a good deal. It was like passing the jerk test. But if the guy nodded as if he already knew all about the Chester standards, Dave would let loose with the zinger: "Look," he'd say, "I can't tell you anything you don't know about what we sell. All I can do is recommend this model, right here." He'd point to the piece of equipment with the most lights on it . . . which was usually very expensive, but not particularly good. "As I'm sure you've read, it's got the best LPD factor available in the market right now."

And the guy would *always* buy it. While he was paying, another salesman or two would give him the thumbs up and say, "Good choice, dude. Excellent LPD factor."

Look in any stereo manual or magazine, and you won't find any mention of the LPD factor. It doesn't exist. One of the salesmen made it up, and it stands for "lights per dollar." Using it was a way of making fun of customers who were so shallow that they worried more about what stereo equipment looked like than how it sounded.

■ ■ ■

Actually, that's not right. The LPD factor *does* exist, and you see examples of it every day. It comes with the handbag that cost four times what you really wanted to spend; it's a part of those jeans that are expensive because they carry the label that everyone wants to wear. The LPD factor is why a five-dollar trucker's baseball cap with a goofy logo sells like hotcakes for sixty dollars.

Simply put, the LPD factor is the difference between what you buy because you need it and what you buy to impress other people. That difference can seem bigger—and much more expensive—when you're an adult, but it's something you'll come across your whole life.

For me, the LPD factor kicked in when I was in fourth grade, and every kid at Ox Ridge Elementary School became obsessed with Wacky Packs. They were stickers sold in a pack with gum; kind of like Pokémon cards, but without the annoying TV show or the toys. The pictures on Wacky Packs were just dumb little joke versions of the packaging of everyday products: instead of Band-Aids, one Wacky Pack sticker showed "Band Aches," and instead of Cap'n Crunch cereal, they had "Cap'n Crud." Stuff like that. They were usually just gross enough to be funny to ten-year-olds, you know?

As with most fads—like Pokémon, snap bracelets, and the Spice Girls—it's hard to explain afterwards why we went so crazy over Wacky Packs. The best I can do is say they seemed cool for a while, and having them made *us* cool. So we all bought as many as we could. We spent our allowances, or washed cars or cut lawns to actually earn the money we were blowing on not-very-funny stickers. Bragging about our collections and trading for the stickers we didn't have ate up most of our free time, and caused more than a few friendships to suffer. Wacky Pack collecting wasn't a hobby as much as it was a contest.

Wacky Packs were popular for about a year, and then, overnight, they became very *un*cool. Binders filled with the stickers that took months to collect went from an honored place on the desk to a hiding place under the bed.

You know that scene in *Willy Wonka & the Chocolate Factory* where Charlie's math teacher asks the class how much money they've spent looking for the Golden Ticket hidden in a Wonka wrapper? Our teacher, Mr. Mac, did the same thing to us about a month after the Wacky Pack fad died. When we figured out just how much money we'd blown on stickers that we no longer even looked at, we were stunned, and more than a little embarrassed.

Of course, that didn't stop us from blowing our savings on the yo-yo fad a year later—everyone seemed to need ten of them—and then on the records, T-shirts, and posters of a rock band named Kiss two years after that. Fads exist to make kids give up their money.

By the time it was considered really pathetic to own anything with the Kiss logo on it, most of us started looking for status in the clothes we wore. Wacky Packs, yo-yos, and Kiss albums piled up in the back of the closet while we saved up for expensive polo shirts with little alligator logos and Puma sneakers.* The cost of being cool kept rising.

That's how it works as you get older: The cost of being cool goes up. Having the right shirts and sneakers becomes wearing the right watch, owning the right car, and living in the right neighborhood, hopefully in the nicest house on your block. When you devote your life to trying to impress others, what you spend your money on changes over the years . . . but the reason you're spending it really doesn't.

It's the LPD factor. The easiest way to impress people is by buying stuff. Stuff that will make you look stylish or smart or just plain cool. That's not entirely a bad thing, because impressing other people is good for your self-esteem. Wanting other people to like you or approve of you—or even to think you're cool—is about as basic as eating or sleeping.

The problems start when the *only* way you can think of to win approval is through what you wear or own, and not from who you are. You are so much more than your stuff.

If I asked you to tell me about your best friends, would you give me a list of all the designer labels they wear?

---

*This goes to prove my theory that fashion is on a thirty-year cycle: What did my daughter Anna beg me for, last year? Vintage Puma sneakers

Would you tell me where they shop? Of course not. You'd tell me what they're good at, what makes them laugh, maybe what they like to do. You'd tell me about *them,* not their clothes and possessions. Those things are just stuff. Stuff, when you think about it, isn't really that important.

I wrecked a Chevy station wagon when I was nineteen. Middle-of-the-day, rain-slicked street . . . me driving too fast and not paying enough attention to the car in front to see that it was suddenly slowing down. By the time I noticed, it was too late: I hit the brakes and tried to steer away, but only managed to slide sideways. My side of the car slammed into the other car's rear bumper, and my head hit the window. When the ambulance came, it was quickly determined that everyone else was fine, and I didn't have much more than a nasty headache.

In other words, I was going to live long enough for my father to kill me. (Which he would definitely do just as soon as he found out what I'd done to his car.) The ambulance guys took me to the hospital, where they said I had a mild concussion. I told the doc I was pretty sure I'd be back—in much worse shape—when my dad was done with me. I was kidding . . . or at least I hoped so.

I don't remember who picked me up from the hospital that day. I just remember that it was a long ride home, and my dad called me into the den as soon as I got in. "You okay?" he asked, and I launched right into how sorry I was about the car. He put his hand up, telling me to stop talking. "Cars we can replace," he said. "Kids, we can't."

That's all my dad ever said about that car. Now, because my father is the person that he is, I spent the next ten years getting minilectures every time the forecast called for rain. But you know what? I never minded those lectures, because when it really mattered, when something bad *had* happened, he made it clear what was important. I was. The car could be replaced. The car was stuff.

Too many people don't understand that: they think we're put on the earth to take care of our stuff, rather than letting our stuff make our lives easier or better. My friend Mark's dad collected rare books, and he kept them in a glass bookcase in his study. It stood in a corner that never got sunlight, because Mark's dad didn't want the dust jackets to fade. He only handled his books with special cotton gloves.

In ninth grade, Mark and his class did a project on Charles Dickens. He knew that his father would never let him bring in his first edition of Dickens' *Great Expectations,* which had been published in three volumes in 1861, but he didn't see the harm in carefully taking the books out of the case and photographing them so his class could see what popular novels looked like in the nineteenth century. (This one had ads in it!) Mark mounted the photos on a big sheet of poster board and wrote detailed captions for each one. He saved room on one corner of his project to write a little dedication: "To my father, who taught me to appreciate fine books." He got an A, which his teacher wrote in red marker, just above the dedication.

Knowing Mark, I suspect that an A didn't happen too often. So when he brought that project home to show his dad, he was just about bursting with pride. His dad took one look at it . . . and blew up at him.

How could you take that book out of the case without asking, his father wanted to know. How could you be so stupid? Were you trying to impress your friends? Mark's father looked at the project for about one second—just long enough to get good and mad—and then he took the better part of a half-hour going over the Dickens volumes, making sure Mark hadn't creased, smudged, or damaged them in any way. When he was satisfied that Dickens was unharmed, he gave Mark a second blast. "I'm so disappointed in you," he said. The dedication and the grade were never mentioned.

Mark took the project—which had taken him hours to put together and which he had been so excited to show his dad—back to his room, and slowly tore it up.

Can you imagine any book so valuable that you'd crush someone's spirit just for touching it? Can you think of anything you might own one day that could be more important than your own kid's feelings? Neither can I.

■ ■ ■

It can be great to have nice things. In a funny way, though, it can be even better *not* to have them. Possessions, especially expensive ones, have a way of tying you down. They become burdens, because you have to take care of them and worry about them. Actually, that's just as true of the cheap stuff you accumulate over the years: the CDs you can't seem to part with even though you never listen to them anymore, the little collections of beanie babies or snow globes. All of this stuff adds up to boxes and boxes, which you will one day look at and say, "Well I *can't* get rid of them; they're my memories."

But you know what? They're not. Your memories are in your head, where you don't have to box them up or make space for them. Your memories don't weigh you down like your stuff does. And your memories don't need care and maintenance like your stuff does, maintenance that means time away from the people and places that could be providing you with *new* memories.

This is a hard thing to grasp, believe me; I didn't even start to get it until I hit my 30s and began to purge my apartment (and my parents' basement) of the stuff I'd saved since junior high. Old bowling trophies, varsity letters that I earned by managing teams, crates of old albums I hadn't listened to in years. All of it went. My little collections of things were donated to charity, along with a closetful of clothes I never wore but couldn't seem to part with. I ached a little, watching all of my stuff go . . .

And then, oddly enough, I felt lighter. In a way, those things had been holding on to me just as tightly as I was holding on to them. They kept me focused on my past—and not looking toward whatever was next. All the space in my life that was taken up by things I wasn't really interested in anymore was suddenly open: for new interests and, yes, for new stuff. I even kept some things, but they had more to do with what I wanted to pursue in life and not what I wanted to look back at. And if those pursuits change—if I find myself no longer interested in collecting movies or bootlegged CDs of Elvis Costello concerts—I'll be cleaning out once again.

There's one other benefit to getting rid of stuff once in a while. It makes it harder for people to make easy judgments about you. Think about it: you judge people by their stuff all the time. The girl who still has all her Barbies even though she's thirteen? Immature. Your friend's dad who has a drawer full of expensive watches? Pretentious jerk. The lady next door with the collection of cow-shaped kitchen utensils? What*ever.*

Well, people do the same thing to you. Most will take a look around your room and size you up based on the ~~Johnny Depp~~ ~~Justin Timberlake~~ Ashton Kutcher posters, or the shelf filled with porcelain animals, or what's in your collection of CDs. They'll do that out of laziness; it's much easier to hang a label on you based on what you surround yourself with than it is to take the time to get to know you.

Which leaves you with two choices: surround yourself with things that you're passionate about, so people will get some clues about who you are; or don't surround yourself with much at all, so people will have to look deeper.

The ones that don't want to look deeper? The people who would rather label you based on your stuff? Repeat after me: they're s-h-a-l-l-o-w, and probably not worth your friendship. Send those people to my friend Dave— he's got a special piece of stereo equipment to sell them.

I hear it has an excellent LPD factor.

CHAPTER TWO

FATE

*...A*nd as the music swells to a crescendo, *the lovers spot each other across the aisle. Can it be? They've come full circle, and been brought back together by Chance. Of all of the trains in all of the world, they've both chosen this one. This car. This row. As they reach for each other, arms open to receive their one true love, their soul mate—just at that moment when it's clear to all that they're destined to be together for all time, that they can no longer fight what was meant to be, an odd commotion erupts...*

That's just me, storming up the theater aisle and heading for the box office to ask for my money back.

There's no other way to say this: fate irks me. First of all, it makes for incredibly lazy plotting. Every hack in Hollywood relies on divine intervention when actual inspiration fails them, and so we have an endless stream of romantic movies that hinge on chance encounters and phony "sudden realizations" on the part of star-crossed lovers. These movies tick me off. Yes, I know; I've sat through a million dopey action flicks with plots of equal (or greater) laziness, but I've never taken *that* dopiness quite as personally. Well, there's a reason.

Romance is important. Essential, even. Explosions are not. And because romance is important, it's a crime when it's evoked lazily . . . which is why the notion of fate is so upsetting. Fate, if you think about it, is the opposite of romance.

Quick: which sounds more romantic to you, the lovers who are together because it's "meant to be," or the lovers who strive and claw and build and question and come to the realization that *because* of that struggle, *because* they devoted the time and the effort to learn from and about each other, they've built a love strong enough for a lifetime? It's awfully ironic that the idea of lovers fated to be together is considered romantic. What's romantic about a complete lack of effort or free will? If it's truly fate, and the lovers couldn't possibly do anything to stay away from each other, doesn't that mean that they're not really responsible for being together in the first place?

As I write this, everyone seems to be talking about the effects of entertainment on kids. We parents worry that seeing so much sex in movies and on television will cause our children to run out and have some. We also wonder if shoot-'em-up videogames are inspiring violent rampages in schools. These are worthwhile things to debate, and I've heard thoughtful opinions on all sides. There's one effect of pop culture that isn't much argued about, though, and I suspect that's because no reasonable person would deny it: pop culture creates lofty (and wrongheaded) expectations about love. Like the idea that fate brings people together, or the notion that there's a knight-in-shining-armor coming for you, and all you have to do is wait for him.

But even if you already know that the whole knight thing is silly (and sexist), I worry that pop culture might con you into believing that love is all about the search for a soul mate. That there's a one-and-only person out there who is perfect for you in every way. Maybe part of you will be convinced that love is something that hits you from across a crowded room, that happens "at first sight." If you wind up believing that, get ready for some pretty serious disappointment.

Infatuation is what happens across a crowded room, and I hope you experience that early and often, because it's wonderful. Infatuation can even lead to love, if you're lucky, but it's not often reliable or even terribly real. Some people believe infatuation—an immediate and strong attraction to someone—is biological; it's the human version of the mating instinct. Others think that we react to attractive people the way we react to magnificent art; the symptoms of infatuation are really just the appreciation of beauty. (I've never stammered or felt my hands go clammy in front of a Degas, so I guess I don't agree with that.)

Whatever causes it, infatuation is temporary at best. It only really exists in that little bit of time when you first know someone . . . before you actually learn anything about them. Before you find out that their laugh bugs you, or their wardrobe scares you, or any one of a million things that can dampen your interest. Infatuation wears off. When that happens, and two people have to deal with each other on realistic, everyday terms, it's not uncommon for infatuation to be replaced by disillusionment. Makes sense, really, when you consider that infatuation *is* an illusion.

When someone is right for you—right in the sense that you share enough in the way of values and interests to be suited to each other—infatuation can transform into passionate commitment. *That's* the kind of love you can have some faith in, because you know what it's built on. The kind of love that comes like a bolt from the blue can leave just as dramatically. There's a saying about that last phenomenon, and it's this: "What the hell was I thinking?"

I don't for a moment mean to say that there aren't such things as soul mates; there are, but they're made, not born. The status of soul mate is a destination, not a starting point. It's only when two people have grown accustomed to each other, and then nurtured and shaped by each other that their souls can be said to be "mated." And because the mating of souls is a process, it can happen more than once over the course of your life.

Let's move away from love and soul mates for a moment, and talk about fate in general. Take astrology. (Please.) Plenty of people believe that there's something in the way the stars line up in the galaxy that affects their day. Like, if Saturn is in Jupiter's third moon to the left, then it's a bad time to try to talk to that boy they like. Or if Venus and Mars aren't in sync, they'll have a screaming match with their boss. They believe this because some fraud with a newspaper column and a sky chart tells them so.

Let me say this delicately. If you start to believe that the rise of Mercury can affect your head, then you've got your head up Uranus. Astrology, like tarot card readings and the psychic telephone hotline, is nonsense created to separate foolish people from their money. And to give the weak-willed an excuse for their failings.

I know, I know . . . I'm being harsh. It's just that I want you to believe in yourself, and not write your failures—or successes, for that matter—off to some great cosmic power, whether you call that power fate or astrology or simply dumb luck. None of those things control your life. *You do.* The path of your life isn't forced upon you; your "fate" is what you get to shape every day by what you choose to do or not do. I think what happens to so many people is that they become overwhelmed with those choices; they're so afraid of making a *wrong* choice about the direction of their life that they make *no* choice . . . and then they sit there paralyzed, trying to convince themselves that their unhappiness isn't their fault. It's fate's fault.

One spring break, my college roomies and I got cheap airfare to a resort island near the equator. We brought sun-

27

screen, a boom box, and Billy, one roommate's nineteen-year-old brother, who at the time was sort of between colleges. Billy was laid-back and funny, and all of the girls we met on the island loved his whole bohemian act. His musical taste ran to hard-core party bands, like the Dead and Santana, and his wardrobe was early thrift shop. He considered himself an artist, and though he was not yet a very good one, he kept telling anyone who would listen that he'd never sell out and paint for money. He was cool in every way that it's possible to be cool at the end of your teens, including the way he rejected both structure and authority. The boys wanted to hang out with him, the girls dug him, and I couldn't have been more jealous.

He didn't much like me, either, and went out of his way to poke fun at me whenever anyone else was around. At the time I took that as inevitable; he saw me as uptight and felt the need to deflate me. Our mutual hostility boiled over a bit one night as a group of us walked along the beach, when someone looked up at the constellations and mentioned astrology.

Billy believed in it, and I pounced. His argument had something to do with the staying power astrology has had; as if the fact that folks had believed in it for centuries made it true. I pointed out that the world has largely held women inferior for most of its history, and yet those of us on the beach that night considered ourselves enlightened on that score. (That's called shamelessly playing to the audience;

28

I'm not proud.) He changed course and argued that I lacked the imagination to understand cosmic order, and I attacked him right back by saying that he lacked the intelligence to pick such nonsense apart. Of course, being boys, debate gave way to name-calling, each of us now sure that the other was a complete jerk.

A few days later, Billy got into another argument, this time with a stranger: an American painter who now made his living selling his artwork to tourists at the various beach resorts. Billy made the mistake of doing his "I would never sell out *my* art by painting for money" routine in front of the guy, and the guy let him have it. In front of a bunch of well-off, basically selfish kids, the painter told Billy what a well-off, basically selfish kid he was, and how lofty pronouncements about "selling out" are usually made by those who've never had to lift a finger to keep themselves fed. Or on Aruban vacations, for that matter. Billy protested (mostly after the painter had left) that true art demands purity of motive, and so great artists are *fated* to be unsuccessful during their lifetimes . . . but we all knew he'd been made a fool of.

Years later I realized that I shouldn't have been so gleeful when Billy got chewed out; I should have had a little compassion for him. In a way, Billy already saw himself as a failure, and was using fate in its many forms as a dodge for the things he didn't think he could accomplish. Not staying in school or finding a livelihood? It was his fate. He wasn't *meant* for those things. Not finding a paying gig as an artist? It wasn't his fault; he was just not going to compromise himself by becoming commercial. If he never found success with his painting, he seemed to say, it would merely prove the purity of his art. *That's the way it goes for true artists: can't fight fate.*

Believing in fate is like leaving the bat on your shoulder and never swinging at a single pitch; it's giving up before you've even tried. I wrote a few pages back that love wouldn't have a whole lot of value if it was dictated by forces outside of our control, and I'd say the same for living. If you really have nothing to do with how your life turns out—if it's all decided by some unseen hand of fate—then how can you take any pride in your accomplishments? Believing in fate means missing the most basic truth about life: *you* are responsible for you. If you want to be fulfilled, you have to get out there and figure out what will fulfill you. If you want to be happy, you have to make your own happiness.

Life is a series of possibilities. There are so many paths you can walk down, and what makes life so exciting and unpredictable is that *you* get to choose which path. Realize that you can change course when the need or the mood arises; this is great to know when you're messing up royally. Have some patience with yourself, and know that what's so wonderful about the false starts is this: the very fact that you recognize them as false starts, the fact that

30

you've been able to correct yourself, is proof that life really is what *you* make it, and not what's been laid out for you.

Maybe one of these days I'll check in on Billy. I hope that he pursued art, because he had a lot of promise. I hope that, whatever he's doing, he no longer believes in fate. I hope that he believes in himself.

CHAPTER THREE

BEAUTY

In Hollywood, there is only one woman who matters: the skinny blond woman with perfect breasts. She's on every magazine cover and in every television show. Go ahead, walk by the newsstand, and check out this month's *Maxim* or *Cosmopolitan*. Look at the covers of *Glamour* and *Teen Vogue*. Betcha ten bucks that most of what you'll see is exactly what I described: skinny blonds. Are there a few brunettes among them? Maybe . . . but I guarantee their chests are perfect, too.

Why is this so, when women come in so many wonderful colors, looks, shapes, and sizes? It's because most of the people who make entertainment are businessmen, not artists. They want to sell as much of their product as they can, whether it's magazines or movie tickets or CDs, and the easiest way to do that is to produce things that appeal to the greatest number of people at the same time. In other words, things that appeal to people with pretty average taste. If the entertainment industry were an ice cream store, it would only sell one flavor: vanilla.

And so we're surrounded by skinny women with perfect breasts. They are the singers in the pop bands, the actresses on the screen, the women hosting the shows, the models on the magazine covers. Sometimes they're many of those things at once, like Jessica Simpson. Take away Jessica's looks, and would she have been the star of her own MTV reality show or a successful singer? Would companies like Pizza Hut have written her big checks to push their products? Not likely.

Women like Jessica Simpson are really successful because they're human Barbie dolls. Amazing hair, faultless features, lots of makeup, hourglass figure. They fit Hollywood's idea of the perfect woman, and so they're given record contracts and TV shows and commercial deals. What *you're* given is an inferiority complex: if Jessica Simpson is the perfect woman, physically, and you don't look like her, that must mean that you are somewhat less than perfect. Right?

Wrong. For starters, even Jessica Simpson doesn't look like Jessica Simpson without a team of experts who do her hair, her makeup, her physical training, her wardrobe fittings, and her lighting. This idea of "perfection" that we're sold can't be found in nature. It's created only after thousands of dollars have been spent *altering* nature. I don't use the Barbie doll comparison by accident: by the time Hollywood is done making women over, they often look like they're made of plastic.

• • •

And they're often just about as healthy as a hunk of plastic. This is why I resent Hollywood so much for selling its beauty obsession to teenaged girls: at exactly the time when you should be concentrating on how your body *works,* they're busy convincing you that the only thing that matters is how it *looks.* So instead of choosing a balanced diet to make yourself strong, you might be tempted to choose a minuscule diet to make yourself skinny.

It's a freaky thing, watching your own body develop. For boys it's a little easier, because our proportions don't usually change all that much. Yeah, our voices crack, and some of us start sprouting peach fuzz on our faces, but the day-to-day differences aren't all that dramatic. For you, though . . . well, I can't imagine. One day—bam!—you've got breasts. And your hips keep getting wider until suddenly your mother stops talking about your body and starts talking about your "figure." It feels like everyone notices. To make the experience extra special, the boys in your social circle will feel free to provide a running commentary on all the changes you're going through, complete with gross terms for your breasts and your butt.

Not all of the changes happen at exactly the same time, so you might find yourself feeling top (or bottom) heavy for a while. Maybe you'll grow a little bit of a belly to go with your chest and your hips, even though you're eating the same amount of food you always have. Maybe no matter what you eat, you find yourself getting thinner. It helps to think of the whole development thing as a process; you go in looking like a girl, and you'll come out at the other end looking like a woman. The stuff in the middle is just what everyone goes through, and it's almost never much fun.

That's not to say that there's nothing you can do to help your body along as it develops. What they tell you in school is absolutely true: it's all about diet and exercise. Eat a balance of stuff . . . get protein, carbohydrates *and* a bit of fat in your diet, because the one thing most nutrition experts agree on is that your body needs all of it. I can't tell you how many women I know that have tried to stop eating fat altogether, and then scratched their heads when they don't get lighter. That's because when you deprive your body of something completely, it goes into a kind of shock and stops burning off the stuff you *are* eating. The trick is portion control. Eat balanced meals until you're satisfied, and then stop.

Actually, eat until you're satisfied, and then go *move*. If you think of food as fuel, it makes sense that you have to burn it off. When you run, dance, work out, or whatever it is you like to do that gets your heart going, you're helping your body develop into something fit and strong. You have to give the body fuel, and then you have to use it; both ends of that equation are equally important. Diet and exercise.

Now, if you try to take a shortcut to a healthy body and decide that you're going to stay thin by not eating, a bunch of things will happen. First, you won't have to worry about exercise, because you won't have the energy for it. Then, you'll watch as your skin starts to age too quickly, because it's not getting what it needs from your diet. Same with your hair. Oh, and you probably won't have to worry about your chest or your hips getting womanly dimensions, because those things rely on nutrition, too.

Does any of this sound attractive to you? Looking like a skinny boy with bad skin and hair? (Which, come to think of it, perfectly describes *me* at the age of fourteen. I wouldn't wish my teenage looks on *anybody*.) If it does sound good, you may as well take up smoking, too, to make sure your teeth and lungs match the rest of you. Sure, you'll greatly increase your chances of dying young . . . but you'll leave behind a skinny corpse!

For just a moment, do what Hollywood can't seem to do: think about your body in terms of what you want it to do, and put aside how you want it to look. Do you like to dance? Play softball? A strong, healthy body will help you with just about anything you can dream up, from skiing to hiking to team sports to—when you're ready for it—making love. Whatever your body can do, it can do much better if you're in shape.

And yes, concentrating on staying healthy will make your body more attractive. Being fit helps you avoid becoming too fat or too skinny, and if you're already at one of those extremes, diet and exercise can help you come back.

I met a lady a few months back who was very heavy and

very proud of it. "I'm a big, beautiful woman," she told me, which was a phrase she'd learned from an online support group. I smiled and agreed with her. She was definitely big, and she was beautiful. But what I should have done is said, "Yes, ma'am, you are . . . and you're headed for a big, beautiful coffin, because I just watched you climb one flight of stairs and you're huffing and puffing like you went ten rounds with the heavyweight champ of the world." In her way, she was every bit as misguided as the folks who starve themselves to stay skinny. She was completely focused on how her body appeared, not on how it worked.

Or what was inside of it. That's the *other* problem with focusing on your looks: you wind up attracting people who are also focused on your looks, and probably on their own. That's swell if you plan on looking at each other all day, but it doesn't bode well for interesting conversation—or any real emotional attachment.

You are so much more than the shell you inhabit. It's easy to forget that when boys flock toward girls who are beautiful and who have curves. It's easy to envy that kind of attention or, if you're the one receiving it, to think it's the best thing in the world. But dig deeper; think about what qualities you value most in other people.

Do you like people who are smart? Funny? Who are good listeners? Or is the way they look more important than any of these things? If it is, then chances are good that you'll date people who prize the same thing, and whose feelings about you will be directly related to what their eyes take in. If you have a bad hair day, their interest in you will lessen. If you break out in zits or gain a few pounds, or if any one of a million things that can affect your exterior happens, you'll risk losing them. If they find someone prettier, get ready for the old adios. Beauty is a fragile thing, and so are relationships based on it.

On the other hand, your personality, your intelligence, and your sense of humor are not things that can change so readily, and if those are things that other people find attractive about you, you can be a little more secure about yourself *and* the people you attract.

I remember thinking in junior high and high school that the kids who were really good-looking had it made. Teachers treated them better, the rest of us fought for their company—the world seemed to revolve around them. Beauty was a blessing, and those of us that weren't so blessed were drawn to the kids who were . . . even though we were so jealous of them we could barely see straight. I remember thinking (bitterly) that their lives would always be effortless and perfect.

And then I got to know two very beautiful roommates in college; both good students, both nice enough girls. Tory—short for Victoria, a regal name that fit her—had come from one of those Midwestern, all-American high schools you see in John Hughes movies, like *Sixteen Candles* or *The Breakfast Club*. She'd lived the whole "popularity" thing and dated jocks. She'd been in *Seventeen* magazine in a silly "Fabulous Hair!" photo collage. We had a European history class together, but I couldn't seem to work up the nerve to talk to her. She was too beautiful.

Late in the semester, we were assigned a project together—I could have kissed the professor for pairing us—and I finally had a chance to get to know her. That beauty that had put me off? Turns out it wasn't doing her any favors, either. As we became friends and I got to watch her in different situations, I learned a little something about how looks can be a curse as well as a blessing. Where I had to fight to get girls to notice me, she had to fight to get guys (including that professor) to take her seriously. She had to fight to get other girls past their instant jealousy and to like her. She had to wonder about the motives of the guys who asked her out . . . did they genuinely want to get to know her, or did they want to impress their friends?

Don't get me wrong; it's not like I felt sorry for her. I just stopped seeing physical beauty as the winning ticket in the instant lottery of life. I noticed that Tory had to sort of play down her beauty, so that she could accomplish the things that were important to her.

Her roommate, Claudia, went the other way. She'd come to Northwestern from a town in Northern California, where she'd been considered pretty, but not gorgeous. As happens with some people, though, she sort of *became* gorgeous overnight: she got herself into shape, got a great haircut, and learned (from Tory) how to put makeup on better.

It was fun, watching Claudia's transformation; it was like one of those scenes in a movie where the plain Jane becomes a real beauty. (The makeover scene in *The Princess Diaries* comes to mind, but for my money Anne Hathaway was just as lovely before they went to work on her as she was after.) For Claudia, the physical change was life-altering. Her social life went into hyperdrive. She broke up with the guy she'd been dating at home and became a "little sister" at three different frat houses.

Even though Tory kept at her to do her class work, Claudia grabbed on to all the things her beauty brought her and started to neglect the rest. The stuff she talked about got less and less interesting, and the word "I" became the main thing in her vocabulary. The friends she had made in her dorm began to avoid her; they all had more important things to think about than the next formal dance. Even Tory lost touch with her when Claudia moved into a sorority in junior year.

When I got married, I got a nice note from Tory, who saw our wedding announcement in a newspaper. She was married herself, she wrote, and she worked for a law firm that let her work for political candidates; she was still pursuing the stuff she'd been interested in at college. The best part of her letter was that she sounded very happy to be busy and very much in love with the guy she'd wed. (The picture she sent showed that he was nice looking, but he wasn't ever going to be on the cover of *GQ*.) She asked me to update her on my roommates and wondered if I'd ever heard anything about Claudia. I wrote back and told her I hadn't.

Which is how it stayed for another ten years. Then, long after I'd forgotten all about Claudia, I met her again at a beach party in East Hampton, New York. You know what? She still isn't interesting. She still uses "I" more than any other word. The only difference I could find is that she's become incredibly insecure. In the span of about ten minutes, she told my wife about her "boob job," her other plastic surgery, and her four-hundred-dollar haircuts. She also took one look at our host's babysitter, a lovely college girl, and said, "No way would I let my husband anywhere near *her*."

Of course she wouldn't. Claudia's world, where physical beauty is more important than brains or character, must be a scary place for a woman who no longer looks as young and sexy as Claudia did in college. If her beauty was the main thing that attracted her husband, she must lie awake at night wondering if he'll stick around when she's no longer quite so beautiful. She must be terrified that their relationship is only skin deep.

The world is full of Claudias. It never occurs to them that the people worth having in their lives care a lot more about what's in their hearts than what they look like in a bathing suit. So folks like Claudia keep plastic surgeons and diet doctors in business, until they eventually become bitter old people who look jealously upon anyone younger and prettier than they are. In other words, they become ugly.

And I'm not talking about their faces.

CHAPTER FOUR

BOYFRIENDS

(Or Three Simple Rules for Dating, My Teenage Daughter)

I have to go get fingerprinted.

See, in New York City, owning a big ol' pump-action shotgun requires a license, which requires fingerprinting, so I have to go get it done. Then I'll be ready when the first boy comes to my door to pick up one of my daughters for a date. I want him to find me sitting in my chair, oiling up the barrel. That way he'll be in the right frame of mind when I ask the question, "What time were you planning on having her home, son?" Maybe I'll jack a round into the chamber (with that satisfying *chick-CHICK* noise) just for effect.

Just about every father of a teenage girl in the world has had a similar thought: substitute the words pistol, hunting knife, sword, or heat-seeking nuclear device for shotgun, and I figure you have all of us dads covered. We live in fear of your dating. We know boys—we *were* boys—and now that we're the old guys in the situation, we have a pretty good idea of exactly what goes through the minds of the young guys. So we fantasize about arming ourselves.

What we don't know, of course, is what goes on in *your* mind. We didn't then and we don't now. That's why we can't ever seem to give you enough credit for being able to take care of yourself. But don't hold that against us, because no matter how terrible we are at conveying it, we really do just want you to be happy and safe. Even if that means we have to *remove* a few boys along the way. (Sorry. The "I'm gonna hunt down and kill any boy that tries to touch you" joke is an automatic thing for fathers. The best version ever is in the movie *Clueless,* when Alicia Silverstone's father tells a boy, "Anything happens to my daughter, I've got a .45 and a shovel. I doubt anybody would miss you.")

It doesn't help us dads that we barely even recognize the boys who show up at the door. What's with the gobs of hair product . . . are all those sharp, gel-created points on their heads meant as some bizarre form of self-protection? And is it really necessary to wear pants so baggy that they would safely hold a family of five? Boys look so different from what we looked like at their age that it confuses us; it makes us wonder what else it is we don't know about the boys you hang around with.

Most of all, though, we're freaked out by the boys that you'll go out with because they represent the beginnings of your independence. Deciding who you'll date is maybe the first big decision you'll make entirely without us. (Oh, we'll try to make suggestions, but you won't listen. And you'll be right not to. Mostly.) We look at these boys who come into our homes—and your life—and we search them for clues about *you*. About what you're looking for and what kind of woman you'll become. In some ways, your choices about boys tell us more about you than anything else.

So have a little patience with your dad, okay? This dating stuff is hard on us.

It's no picnic for you, either, because while we're getting all weird and making jokes about shotguns, you're taking your first steps toward romantic relationships . . . and as often as not, those steps feel like they're taking place in a minefield. How do you know if you're choosing the right guys? Why don't they just come out and tell you what they're thinking, like your girlfriends do? How serious should you let yourself get with someone?

These are all things you're going to have to sort out for yourself, but that doesn't mean your folks can't give you a *little* guidance. As tempting as it will be for me to comment on every boy who comes through my door, I'll try to hold my tongue . . . except, that is, for offering three little rules that might make the dating minefield a little more manageable.

*

First, make sure that you date boys because you honestly like them. Duh, right? Well, as obvious as it may seem, it's advice a lot of people don't follow. You'll watch plenty of relationships spring up for motives other than romantic attraction. You'll see girls pick guys based on their popu-

47

larity, their car, or any one of a hundred other reasons that have nothing to do with a real spark. And while it's undoubtedly fun dating a guy just because he can spend a ton of money on you, it's also not very smart. When you make money the basis for a relationship, the only important person in that relationship is the one who has the money, you know? You become just another object that money brings, like an MP3 player or great clothes. And, like those things, you'll be replaceable.

* *

Second, date guys within a year or two of your own age. My friend Alana always went out with much older guys. "I was so impressed with their confidence," she told me, "and my friends thought I was really sophisticated, because these guys chose me."

In junior high, she dated high school boys. In high school, she dated college boys. By the time she graduated, she found herself going out with guys a decade older than she was. She also found herself miserable. Because no matter what her friends thought, she *wasn't* that sophisticated, and her boyfriends didn't mind letting her know it. "I always felt inferior, because they seemed to know so much more than I did about *everything,* and while they loved to show me off to their friends, they had no patience around *my* friends." The last straw came when she was having dinner with a thirty-one-year-old lawyer she'd been dating and his friends, and she voiced an opinion about politics.

"No offense," her boyfriend said, "but you're twenty-two. What could you know about it?" He was her ex-boyfriend before dessert was served.

What Alana realized was that relationships are supposed to be about sharing experiences, about learning things together. Looking back at her whole dating life, she suddenly felt stupid. "Everything I was going through, the guys I dated had been through years before me. The stuff they were going through, I was too young for. We had nothing to talk about!"

But while holding a conversation with Alana seemed too challenging for her boyfriends, they didn't have the same problem with sex. Being sexual with them became her way of trying to feel like their equal. It didn't work very well. She lost her virginity to a guy who couldn't wait to take her home as soon as it was over, so he could get back to his friends. "I was *so* not ready, and I got very shaky afterward. He kept saying, 'What's the big deal? It's just sex.' And for him, it was. Been there, done that. For me it was something that should have been incredibly intimate and special, and I threw it away to hang on to a college guy."

Still, she kept dating older guys. Alana had gotten so used to the way they treated her—which was lousy— that she came to believe it was all she deserved. "By college, I had zero self-esteem," she says. "These guys basically wanted me for sex and to show off to their friends . . . and I thought I was lucky! If I had a time machine, I'd go and find myself at the age of fourteen. I'd shake that girl by the shoulders and say, 'Why should guys respect you, when you don't even respect yourself?'"

* * *

Which brings me to the third, most important rule of dating: *make sure that your boyfriends treat you with respect.* Always. If they take you for granted, dump 'em. If they try to pressure you into something you don't want to do, dump 'em. If they ever touch you in any way that isn't invited and affectionate, dump 'em. (Then tell an adult. If you can't tell your folks, tell a teacher or an aunt or anyone with enough experience to help you handle it.)

Ever heard of a zero-tolerance policy? It's a fancy way of saying "no second chances." Zero tolerance is a great rule to have in place when it comes to your love life. That doesn't mean you can't argue with a guy you're dating or even forgive him for being immature at times. What it *does* mean is that no matter what's going on between the two of you—good or bad—you always feel respected. You always feel valued for what *you* bring to the relationship.

If you have to exercise the zero-tolerance policy, and actually dump a guy, you'll feel lonely for a bit. You'll worry that no other boy is going to want to date you because you're such a pain. And yes, the boys you break up with because they don't treat you well *will* tell their friends you're a pain. (Or a bitch, which is the Official Favorite Word of Guys-Who-Treat-Girlfriends-Like-Dirt™.) The thing is, you won't get the reputation you'll worry about

50

getting. At least not among the guys who deserve your time. They'll see a girl who knows what she's worth and isn't willing to accept any less. And deep down in a place most guys don't even know they have, they'll think, "If a girl *that* self-confident chooses me, it must mean *I'm* worth something, too." Any boy who makes that realization is a boy you can bring home to meet your dad.

I'll try to remember to wash the fingerprinting ink off before I shake his hand.

CHAPTER FIVE

SEX

Don't have any, ever. At least wait until I'm dead. Is that so much to ask?

CHAPTER FIVE-A

SEX, REALLY

It's amazing: even though I'm over 40 now, my first impulse when the subject of sex comes up is *still* to crack jokes and laugh nervously. So forgive that last page. I figure I can manage to keep a straight face if you can. Shall we start?

I didn't learn about sex until ninth grade.

Relax. I wasn't *that* clueless. I'd gotten the basic facts down by the time I was eleven, and even had most of them right . . . which is a miracle since I had to learn them from my friends in the playground.

We didn't have much in the way of sex education in public school during the 1970s. Come to think of it, we didn't have it anywhere else either. Church didn't teach us anything about sex, except that it was Wrong, Sinful, and that we Should Not Do It, until we got married. And even then only to have babies, and *For No Other Reason*. The television told us roughly the same thing. Before HBO came along the airwaves were pretty prudish, and when unmarried characters on shows *did* have sex, it always had to have horrible consequences like unplanned pregnancy or disease. (The horror movies that we grew up with, like *Friday the 13th* and *Nightmare on Elm Street,* took that a bit further: the first people to die in those films are *always* the characters who sneak off to have sex. And who's always still alive at the end? The virgin, naturally.)

I did get information from my folks, but it came in a booklet written by a doctor. It was about the mechanics of human egg fertilization, fetal development, and birth. Reading it was about as exciting as reading the directions for building a model airplane . . . and come to think of it, the illustrations were just as thrilling. But believe it or not, the fact that I was handed a booklet put me ahead of most of my friends: their parents believed firmly that if they didn't talk about sex, it wouldn't happen.

Now, parents have evolved a little bit since I was picking up the facts of life in the schoolyard, and we realize that *not* teaching you about the risks of sexually transmitted infections and unwanted pregnancy would be stupid, so we let most schools do that. But pretty much just that. So you have "health" and "issues" classes, where the possible consequences of sex are taught. More specifically, the bad ones.

We—or the school—teach you about disease and pregnancy, and tell ourselves that's "sex education." But where's the sex? What we *don't* teach you about is sex. What it means to be intimate. How it feels, emotionally. What you'll go through when you first start experimenting, sexually . . . and just as important, that it's different from what boys go through.

Unfortunately, our culture isn't nearly as shy as we are in terms of teaching you about sex. You'll see it on television—and I mean, unless your parents have sheltered you really well, you'll see *IT* on television—and you'll find it in the movies and on just about every magazine stand in America. Sex talk. Sex tips. Sex stories. We've got *Maxim* magazine. Music videos. *American Pie* movies. It's all about sex, 24/7, in the bluntest and crudest terms imaginable. While I grew up with songs that talked about having sex in really vague ways (Bob Seger described it as "workin' on mysteries without any clues"), today's singers gleefully describe being caught "bangin' on the bathroom floor." So much for the mystery.

But while the culture has changed, the message you get from us, your folks, hasn't. Don't do it. Don't have sex. Oh, and don't talk to us about it.

When the subject of sex does manage to come up—despite our best efforts—we give you the most bizarrely mixed signals. It's bad to sleep around, we'll say; it's wrong to have sex with lots of different people. We'll say that, and then we'll sit next to you on the couch watching some old *Friends* rerun, laughing our heads off when Joey can't remember the name of the woman he slept with the night before. We'll tell you that oral sex is extremely intimate, and that people shouldn't cheat on their spouses, and then when the president is caught having oral sex with someone he's not married to right in the Oval Office, what do we do? We make jokes about it. It's funny!

So how can you not be confused? You have a lot more to contend with, sexually speaking, than we ever did.

Let's clear up one little bit of confusion before we go on: when I use the word "sex," I'm not just talking about intercourse. I hear more and more people argue that all kinds of intimate things are "okay" because they're somehow not sex, and I shake my head. If the object of something is to stimulate the sex organs, what is it, if not sex? Fishing? Please. Anyone who argues that "it really isn't sex if it isn't intercourse" is either trying to talk you into something that they think you're hesitant to do, or they're trying to save their own hide. (Like that president I mentioned a few paragraphs ago.)

Sex, then, involves what people call their "private parts." Those are the parts of us that we don't share with the world . . . as opposed to our "public parts," like our faces and hands and ankles and elbows, the parts that the world gets to see and touch on a pretty regular basis. When we share our private parts with someone in an intimate way—*any* intimate way—that's sex.

I finally got some useful sex education in ninth grade. In English class.

As part of a homework assignment from Mr. Bouvier,

each of us had to pick a song, write out the lyrics, and give a presentation about what we thought the writer meant by the words. All of us took this as a cheap excuse to play our favorite tunes during English period.

Well, all of us except for Ti. A little introduction: Ti Herrera was a goddess. Still is, actually. She was beautiful, she was kind, she was funny . . . and she talked to me, which at the time seemed miraculous. (Have I mentioned my teenage buckteeth, skinny body, or bad hair yet?) Ti wasn't just drop-dead gorgeous, she was sexy. Understand that I don't mean that in a Britney Spears, lemme-show-you-98-percent-of-my-skin kind of way . . . Ti had a confidence that went with her looks. She seemed worldly in a way that the rest of us were not. She was the first girl that most of us at Middlesex Junior High found sexy.

So when she strolled to the front of Mr. Bouvier's class and handed out a lyric sheet for a song about sex, the boys in third period English just about stopped breathing.

Then we snickered, because that's what kids do when the topic of sex comes up. Ti was about to explain a song—Meat Loaf's "Paradise by the Dashboard Light"—that is so sexually explicit most of us couldn't play it in front of our parents. As you've probably figured out, it's about a couple having sex in a parked car. Ti put the record on. We'd all heard it before, but somehow it seemed even more sexual this time, considering who'd chosen it and the fact that we were sitting in a classroom with a teacher, reading along.

The song is a three-part mini-musical. In the first part, a

man and a woman describe the night they lost their virginity, in a car parked by a lake. "Ain't no doubt about it, we were doubly blessed," they sing, "'cause we were barely seventeen and we were barely dressed." This was, of course, exactly the situation every guy in the class would have liked to find himself in. With Ti.

At the end of the first part of "Paradise by the Dashboard Light," a weird thing happens. The song is taken over by Phil Rizzuto, announcer for the New York Yankees, who gives a play-by-play commentary of what's going on in the car. You've heard your friends talk about sex by "the bases," right? We talked about it that way, too. Anyway, Rizzuto describes how the boy is racing for home plate on a bunt, and what a close play it's going to be. "Holy cow!" he says. "I think he's gonna make it!"

The second part of the song starts with the girl screaming, "Stop right there!" She needs to know where this relationship is going before she agrees to go all the way. "Will you love me forever?" she asks, and the boy tries to stall, singing, "Let me sleep on it, I'll give you an answer in the morning." After a lot of back and forth, the boy gives in and promises he'll love her "'til the end of time," and the girl gives in and has intercourse.

The final part of the song, called "Praying for the End of Time," finds the boy years later lamenting his promise: "It was long ago and it was far away," he sings, "and it was so much better than it is today."

As the record ended, Ti stood. And proceeded to shame

59

every boy in that room, including yours truly. Up and to the moment she started speaking in that English class, I had wanted to *be* the boy in that car. I wanted sex.

Ti, it turns out, wanted love. Though she hadn't yet had sex, she managed to understand the song's message and explain it to us. "Boys use love to get sex, and girls use sex to get love," she said, and though that's an oversimplification, it's got a lot of truth to it. (Steve Martin had a great line about this: "I like to put women on a pedestal," he said, "high up enough so I can look up their dress.") "He lies to her because he wants to have sex with her," Ti told us, "and she lies to herself about what she's going to mean to him if she lets him."

The boys in that classroom stopped snickering. Ti had— probably for the first time in our lives—pointed out to us that sex has as much to do with the need to feel loved as it does with body parts. Ti introduced us to the notion that sex comes with consequences beyond what our parents had warned us about. Emotional consequences. Our *real* sex education had just begun. Before that class, we'd thought of "Paradise by the Dashboard Light" as a naughty, fun little story. Thanks to Ti, though, how could we help but see it as a tragedy?

And how could we help but cringe at the way we talked about sex with each other? I remember feeling ashamed during Ti's presentation at how much I'd loved the Phil Rizzuto part, how I'd laughed at his description of the boy's

60

efforts to reach each "base." Now I began to understand that talking about sex in terms of running the bases was juvenile . . . and maybe something worse.

Are the bases still the same today? When I was a kid, kissing was first, touching above the waist was second, below the waist was third, and intercourse was home plate. This was a one-way thing, because we didn't have bases for what girls might do to *us*. And that's it, really: we thought of sex as something that we did to girls. Sex was a game, and girls were the playing field. *Didja get some? How far didja get? Didja steal third?* Sex, for us, was goal-oriented: you kept going until she stopped you.

Our stupidity didn't end with baseball; we came up with all kinds of clever ways to talk about how far we were getting. Like, if a girl wouldn't let a boy touch her genitals, we'd say he was "stopped at Point Levi's." A few pages ago, I said that sex is sharing our private parts in an intimate way. As a way of being close with someone. Does describing sex as a race around the bases sound like intimacy to you?

I'd love to tell you that Ti's presentation made everything about sex suddenly clear to me. (Mr. Bouvier gave her an A, by the way.) It didn't. I still had to wrestle with urges I didn't completely understand and—eventually—signals from girls that I had no idea how to read. But she did manage to open my eyes about the link between the sex organs and the heart. She got me to wonder what sex felt like emotionally.

Sex, I would learn over the years that followed, is incredible. Sex feels *great*. It is the most intimate thing you can do with another human being. Sex is extremely powerful. Not just in that it can create life—or effectively end it, thanks to diseases like AIDS—but because of what it can make you feel, in your heart.

But there's a catch. Sex loses its power when it's given away, when it's done too freely. Think about it: how can you distinguish a serious relationship from a fleeting one, if you're willing to have sex with everyone you go out with? The secret to the power of sex is exclusiveness: doing it as part of a deeply committed relationship (like marriage . . . hint hint) is a way of giving the other person—and yourself—the greatest gift there is.

But doing it so that a boy will love you . . . or even "like" you . . . is cheating yourself in a dozen different ways. First off, it never works: if the goal for the boy is to have sex, the relationship is effectively over as soon as you've done it. Sure, he might stick around to "score" a few more times, but the thrill of that wears off. And when it does, he's gone. Second, you run a very real risk of being branded a "slut." No, it's not fair that promiscuous girls are called sluts and promiscuous boys are applauded, but that's the way it is. Here's something else that's not fair: when they're looking for serious relationships, boys avoid girls who are thought of as sluts. Those girls seem somehow "dirty" to them. Used. (This kind of unfairness has been around forever . . . or at least since biblical times, when women were first per-

62

ceived as property, and women who were not virgins were looked upon as "damaged goods.")

Most of all, though, having sex too young or too often can lessen the power of sex later on in life. It may seem like an old-fashioned notion, this idea of "saving yourself for marriage," but it's based on a valuable truth: sex is really about discovery . . . of sensation and emotion and the power of feeling connected to another human being in an incredibly special way. That's why they call it "making love."

If you separate out the emotion from the sensation, you're lessening the chances that it will seem special to you down the road. That's why the last line of "Paradise by the Dashboard Light" rings so true and feels so sad. Because the man looking back on his teenage fumblings in the back seat of a car never made the connection between sex and love, he's left feeling that "it was so much better than it is today."

I said a few pages back that our culture is obsessed with showing us sex . . . but that's not quite right. What it shows us is a sort of pretend sex, where everyone is beautiful, everything is available, and there are no consequences. But also, there's no joy! Take a good look at Christina Aguilera's face next time you see one of her raunchier videos. One of the ones where she rolls around the floor wearing not much more than a G-string, purring about how she's "dirrty." There's no happiness in that face, just a kind of cold frankness. What's sexy about that?

What the culture doesn't show us—what it *can't* show us—is real intimacy . . . the only reason to have sex. Our music, our television, and our movies sell sensation, but not the much more deeply satisfying part of sex: emotion.

Where does that leave us? Frustrated. We'll never feel as beautiful or as "sexy" as those people that we see on TV; we'll more than likely never attract such beautiful people, either. We'll never know what it's like to have anyone we want without having to worry about things like pregnancy or disease. We'll never measure up to the images we see every day.

And to that I say . . . "Hallelujah."

Because if you take the time to get it right, if you wait until you're absolutely ready to give yourself to someone else, you'll have better, more fulfilling sex than the folks who produce all those images on television could even imagine. And you'll have it for the rest of your life. "Hooking up" and "fooling around" are for people who don't know any better. Those things diminish the awesome power that sex can have. In fact, when your time comes, don't settle for sex. Anybody can have sex.

When your time comes, make love.

CHAPTER SIX

CRUELTY

My friends' daughter has vitiligo. Ever seen it? It's just a skin disorder that causes white patches where a person doesn't have pigment, the stuff that makes you tan. So Emily's knees and elbows are a little different from the rest of her, which is more noticeable in the summer, when she spends about eight hours of each day in a bathing suit.

Emily came home from camp one day last summer in tears. Finally, after a little prodding, she told her mom that there'd been this boy at camp who'd teased her about her skin. Teased isn't the right word: he tortured her. She was a "freak" he said, and then he said she was "super ugly." He said this stuff in front of other kids, to make it hurt as much as possible.

Her mom reacted like an adult *should* react: she drove to the camp, repeated what the boy said to the guy running the place, and asked what the camp could do to protect her daughter from that kind of cruelty.

Emily's dad, though, reacted like a *guy*. He wanted to

find the boy and pound the crap out of him. He told me what had happened, and I offered to join him: we could take turns. We went on that way for a while, figuring out all the evil things we could do to a kid who would pick on such a lovely, loving girl. (Guys like to fantasize about violent revenge, the more gruesome the better. We've seen way too many movies with either Clint Eastwood or Vin Diesel, depending on our age.)

Anyway, we obviously *didn't* go out and administer a pounding, both because it would have been wrong and because we didn't have to: the camp kicked the kid out. Turns out Emily wasn't his only target that day, and even the counselors had told the camp director that the kid had to go.

In one way, the problem was solved. The boy was gone. But in another way, it wasn't. Emily was now suddenly self-conscious about a condition she's had for a long time. That's what bullies do: they make you feel lousy about *you*, they plant seeds of self-doubt. Emily couldn't understand why this boy who she'd never met before would say such horrible things to her . . . and part of her wondered if everyone else secretly thought the same thing.

I went home and looked at my girls that night, and I tried to think of what I would tell them if they were trashed by somebody the way Emily was. As soon as I had an idea, I wrote it in an e-mail and sent it to her. This is some of what it said:

Dear Emily:

I got tortured as a kid—actually, all the way through high school—because I was one of the skinniest boys around. I won't ever forget, at the age of fifteen, being at a bowling tournament and having this really cute girl from another country club decide it was hysterical to call me "boney-bean," a name her friends picked up and used. Needless to say, my bowling suffered, as did my heart. I couldn't help being skinny. I tried to be a good guy; I listened, I cared what other people thought, I wanted to do kind things . . . but I got made fun of 'cause I didn't weigh enough!

That girl didn't know the first thing about me, just like the creep at camp didn't know you. Yet she felt some need to make me feel small. Why? Why is someone cruel to you, even when you've done nothing to him or her? Why would that jerk at camp decide to pick on you for having vitiligo, something that doesn't affect him, and that you have no control over?

Here's the answer that took me years to really under-stand: people are cruel because they're miserable in-side. That nasty little kid lashed out at you today for one reason. He's in pain. He might be mistreated at home; he might be ignored. He might be so insecure that the only way he knows to make himself feel good is by making other people feel bad. You'll never know his reasons, but I promise you one thing: he's really un-happy. In looking back at the people who caused me pain as a kid, I realize that the well-adjusted ones, the kids who had self-confidence, never ever picked on me. It was the ones who didn't get the love and support that I got, or worse, it was the ones whose parents told them they were worthless that felt the need to drag me down.

You can't possibly understand what it's like to feel you don't matter—like you're no good—because your parents make sure that you know just how very much you do matter. And this kid who picked on you could matter, too, but I'm guessing no one will ever tell him that. I hope they will . . . I hope he eventually stops feeling so insecure, because security is sort of the antidote to meanness.

Love,

Philip (formerly known as "boney-bean")

Of course as cruelty goes, what Emily faced is pretty easy to figure out and deal with: the little brat who says something nasty to you for no apparent reason and then promptly disappears from your life? It hurts, but it's over fast.

What's *not* so easy is when it happens a lot. Especially at a place like school, where you can't exactly get away. And—here's the kicker—when the person tormenting you is supposed to be your friend.

In tenth grade, my friend Tracy started finding notes in

her locker. Sometimes two or three a day, always secretly slipped in while she was in class. They weren't signed. They were clearly in a girl's handwriting, but she didn't recognize it.

Here's what the first few notes basically said: "People think you're a slut. Everybody knows what you've done with a certain boy. I'm your friend. I'm worried about you and thought you should know this stuff." The notes made Tracy a little paranoid; she spent her lunches sitting in the Darien High cafeteria, trying to figure out if anyone was looking at her differently. She didn't want to tell any of her friends, because the notes weren't wrong: she'd been "fooling around" (as she put it) quite a lot with her boyfriend, a senior. She didn't think anyone knew.

Tracy started getting quiet. Not telling her friends meant having no way to ask around, to see if she could find out who the writer was. By the time she decided to show them to me, the notes had gotten worse. There was no longer any mention of being a "concerned friend" by the writer. Now they were all about what a slut she was, and how she ought to avoid certain parties. (One note insisted that Tracy's boyfriend was offering to "share" her with his friends.)

We tried to figure out who her new little pen pal was. We started by looking for a motive: who would gain by embarrassing her or by making her break up with the senior? We could only think of two people—one ex-girlfriend of the senior's and one wannabe girlfriend—but they seemed unlikely, because neither of them was acting weird around her. The people who *were* acting weird around her were the members of her clique; Tracy figured that was just because she'd stopped talking since the notes started.

Tracy was wrong. Her friends were acting weird because they knew all about the notes, and Carla, *her best friend since grade school,* was the one slipping them in her locker.

But not the one writing them. That was the work of Olivia, one of the most popular girls in school. Like Tracy's boyfriend, Olivia was a senior . . . and the strange thing was that she'd never so much as spoken a word to Tracy. We never did find out her motive; could be that she didn't like it when senior guys went out with sophomore girls, could be that she was just an evil witch. Either way, it didn't much matter to Tracy. What mattered—what drove her crazy—was why Carla would help humiliate her.

(Carla and Olivia got caught the old-fashioned way: Olivia was showing her letters to her friends, who were telling their boyfriends, most of whom played football. Me, I was too skinny to play football but I managed the team . . . and you'd be surprised how much a manager hears when he's fixing cleats in the locker room.)

Carla's excuse was predictable: "I didn't know what was in the notes. I was just doing Olivia a favor!" When Tracy got teary, Carla got defensive. "What's the big deal? Grow up. It was just a joke!" Yeah. Being called a slut two or three times a day, anonymously, is *so* funny.

You know what was really going on, of course. Carla saw a chance to maybe be friends with a popular senior,

70

and she was willing to hurt an old friend to do it. Tracy's other friends were too afraid of Olivia to say anything. Sadly, it happens all the time. Afraid to be without a group of friends, Tracy forgave them all.

Boy cruelty can be so much easier to deal with than girl cruelty. Boys are usually pretty direct when they're feeling aggressive. One boy will call another one a name right to his face, or he'll just get to it and throw a punch. (And one punch is usually all that ever gets thrown, in a real fight. Then it's a lot of wrestling until someone steps in and breaks it up. If boys fought the way they do in Vin Diesel movies, we'd all be dead by the end of junior high.) The point is that guys don't tend to be anonymous-note writers.

Maybe that's because the reasons for our aggressions are simple. We're miserable and want to spread the pain around, or we're mad because we feel dissed in some way. So we lash out; the point is to let someone know we're unhappy. Boy stuff tends to blow up and then blow over. It happens, and then it's done, and we're on to something else. I can't tell you how many fights I saw between boys who were back to being friends a day later. It's how we're wired.

You girls are more . . . complex. First off, most of the signals you get—from parents and school and the culture —tell you that as a girl you shouldn't be direct when you're angry. So if someone confronts you with "Hey, what's wrong?" you're likely to grit your teeth and say "Nothing. I'm fine." All that does is make the person who asked you imagine that whatever's wrong is even worse than it probably is. It also makes them frustrated . . . which eventually makes them mad at *you*. (That goes for your friends *and* your parents.)

Second, you're much more likely to be insecure than boys are. How could you not be? Girls are judged much more harshly than boys in all kinds of ways. How attractive you are. How your clothes look on you. Where your clothes come from. How your body looks. Boys deal with a little of this—I mean, I was "boney-bean"—but let's face it: you'll never hear a boy say, "Do you think I should lose five pounds?"

And third, girls are just a lot more socially conscious than most boys. Popularity, which you discovered in third or fourth grade, becomes an obsession by high school. Girls tend to keep track of who's "in" or "out," and for a lot of them, school becomes one long game where the object is to stay with the in crowd. At just about any cost.

Put it all together—the need to avoid confrontation, the insecurity, and the desire to be a part of the social scene—and you have the perfect recipe for some really awful behavior. Friends backstabbing each other. Anonymous notes. Anonymous e-mails. Rumors. Sometimes even open name-calling, but that tends to be done by girls in packs; there's safety—and often a lot of meanness—in numbers.

But here's the good news: you're wired differently from

boys in one other major way. You have the ability to learn from awful experiences, and to make changes that will help you avoid going through the same bad stuff over and over again.

I asked Tracy one night not long after college what had ever happened to Carla. "No idea," she said. She told me the friendship was basically over as soon as she found out that Carla was slipping Olivia's notes in her locker, even though the rest of us thought they put it behind them. "Forgiving her wasn't that hard," Tracy told me. "I felt bad for her. She was so desperate to be popular! I just never trusted her again." In fact, she said, Carla became the focus of nasty whispering within their clique: the girls pointed out to each other how pathetic she was, trying to get in good with the seniors by trashing her friend. (Notice how they conveniently ignored what lousy friends *they* had been, too?)

Tracy, though, didn't join in. She knew what she thought of girls who whispered about each other, and she didn't want to be one of them. She still hung out with her clique, but she slowly made some new friends, carefully avoiding girls who seemed too interested in popularity.

We talked a lot that night about the things kids do to hurt each other. I told her about the jock who spent seventh through ninth grades taunting me, every day, with a comment on how skinny I was. (Until Ed Mellett, the toughest kid in school and one of my best friends, heard him one day and then asked me, in front of a hallway full of kids, if I wanted him to beat the crap out of the guy. "Nah," I said. The fear in the guy's eyes was enough payback for me.)

Then I told Tracy what my mom always said when I came home with hurt feelings: "People only do to you what you let them." Tracy liked that a lot. I'd never really understood it—in fact, I hated when my mom said that because I mistakenly thought it meant I was somehow *asking* to be bullied—but Tracy got it. She understood that my mom was saying both sides have a choice: a bully can choose to say horrible things to you, and you can choose whether or not to take those things to heart.

"I gave those girls *so* much power over me," she said. "I cried every day for *weeks* when I got those notes, and I started to doubt every friend I had. I wasn't doing my schoolwork; I didn't even want to go out at night. And why? Because a couple of cowards thought it would be funny to hurt me. Olivia didn't know anything about me, and she didn't care. Messing with me was just a way to make herself feel powerful."

See a pattern here? The boy who called Emily a freak didn't know the first thing about her either. She let him upset her—she gave him power over her—because she didn't know better. His cruelty was that he made her question her own looks; he made her wonder if he was right about her.

It sucks, being bullied or made fun of. Teachers and parents mean well when they tell you to "just ignore it," but that's a really hard thing to do. Say some girl is taunting you at school. How do you ignore being laughed at in front of a bunch of people, or, like Tracy, finding out that your friends are all calling you "slut" behind your back? You can't *un*hear things.

What you can do, though, is practice what all good journalists know: always consider the source. Think about the girl behind the words or threats. Why would she want to hurt you? If it's because you've done something bad to her first, then apologize. If that's not it, try to understand how completely miserable she must be if the only way she can make herself feel better is by spreading her pain.

Then be really, really glad you're not her.

CHAPTER SEVEN

LETTING GO

I was quite a bowler as a kid. Okay, I wasn't great at it, but I loved it. Not only are you "up" at least ten times a game (as opposed to four or five for baseball), but the chance to improve comes constantly. So does the chance to lose it completely. The distance between a strike and a gutter ball is only a couple of feet.

Most of all I loved bowling because, like all great sports, it's played largely between you and your mind. And your mind will mess with you. Want to know what a mean, conniving little kid I could be? I used to ask other kids, just before their turns, if they breathed in or out when they rolled the ball. So they'd start to think about *that* while they were bowling and not the actual technique of rolling the ball, and it always screwed them up. Then, after knocking down a pathetic three pins on their first ball, they would come up with ways to screw with *my* game. Which, of course, made bowling fun.

Like other games that rely heavily on your mind, bowling has its share of superstitions. None is more powerful than the "stopper." The stopper, used properly, can turn your luck around in one frame, and turn a disastrous game into a respectable one. A stopper, strategically placed, can get you back into winning form. Here's how it works:

Say you're having an awful game; you can't pick up a spare to save your life, and you're splitting the seven and ten pins with alarming regularity. The pins are against you . . . and it's only the fourth frame. What do you do?

You give yourself a stopper. A stopper is just a mark you make on the page where you keep score. It's a line drawn vertically on the right side of the box where you've scored your current frame, which is also the left side of the box where you'll score your next frame. It's just a line that more forcefully separates where you are now (Slumpsville, USA) with where you want to be next time you're up (which is Fat City, baby). A stopper is a way of keeping all the bad luck in the past away from the good luck you'd like to have in the future.

Someone once said that you make your own luck, and that sounds about right. Actually, I don't believe in luck, but I still believe in the stopper. The stopper is nothing more than a cheap psychological trick you play on yourself to refocus your thinking, and nothing less than a miracle. I don't much bowl anymore, but I still use stoppers.

The first time I used one outside of a bowling lane was in college. I'd gotten dumped pretty badly by a woman I was sure was "the one." We'd dated for two years—an eternity when you're 20—and in the end I was less than mature and she was less than faithful. (Never a great combination.) When she called me to her room at the sorority to give me my walking papers, I reacted in a way that would have made any three-year-old proud: I threw a temper tantrum, and pulled apart a stuffed animal I'd given her. (It was Baloo from *The Jungle Book*, and to this day I can't walk into a Disney store and see that blue bear without feeling guilty.) She yelled at me to leave, and in her haste to get her door open, she backed into a mirror propped up against a wall, breaking it.

So imagine the scene: the sorority hallway fills up with girls wondering what the yelling is about, and they see me stalking off, bits of poor Baloo's stuffing trailing in my wake. Then they see my girlfriend, standing by a pile of broken glass and a seriously wounded teddy bear, and crying. In the span of about six seconds I'd gone from a guy who'd gotten dumped rather coldly to a brutish jerk who *deserved* it. Calling that night to apologize made things even worse for me because it gave her the chance, in front of an audience of sorority sisters, to self-righteously tell me how inexcusable my behavior was.

Eventually I'm going to pull three lessons out of this story. The first one is about the importance of self-control. Up and to the point where my inner toddler took over, and I felt the need to show my pain by destroying a present I'd given to the person causing that pain, I was a sympathetic character. I was the good guy. I was the wronged party.

By losing it so completely, though, I lost all that stuff; and I became the bad guy. The hardest thing for me was when my now-former girlfriend lectured me on my behavior. It was hard because I knew that she was right. My behavior *was* inexcusable . . . which made me no better than her.

Anyway, back to my tale of woe:

I went back to my apartment, the memory of the stares of the sorority girls still burning me with shame. I cried. When I stopped crying, I sobbed. Then, for a change of pace, I wept some. This completely freaked my roommates out. (Boys have no idea what to do when *girls* cry; when they see another boy crying, it's like the world has turned upside down.) They took turns trying to talk to me, but I was inconsolable. A woman I thought I would marry had dumped me. I'd lost it so completely that any other girl who might have gone out with me would now run screaming from the Baloo-shredding psycho.

When my roomies left to go to class the next morning, I did what kids (and a surprising number of adults) do when they can't see their way past their problems: I ran away. My dad had let me take the Chevy station wagon to school that year—sweet wheels they were not, but I had a car!—so I got on the highway and headed south, away from Chicago, away from the girlfriend, away from the freaked-out roommates, and away from the sorority girls who knew what I'd done. I had absolutely no destination in mind.

And then, somewhere along a rural road in Indiana, I started to think about what running away would mean. I'd fail my classes. I'd *really* freak out my roommates. I'd panic my parents. Maybe more than all of that, I'd prove to everyone that the tantrum-throwing loser was the real me.

I turned around. I knew it was the right thing to do, but the closer I got to campus, the more my chest tightened. The tears seemed awfully close to coming back. I saw a motel sign that advertised a cheap rate, and decided I could afford one night away from everyone that I knew. And it was there, in a crappy motel by the side of the road, that Oprah made everything okay.

Yep. That Oprah.

She'd just come to Chicago to host a local morning show that hadn't been doing too well in the ratings. As I flipped through the channels in that motel—after another lousy night's sleep—I found her talking to her studio audience about some problem or other . . . I had no real interest in (or memory of) what the topic was. Didn't matter. I was mesmerized. Here was this feisty, real, funny person, not letting people get away with feeling sorry for themselves. Making jokes . . . in an oddly supportive way. For a good half-hour, I didn't think about my girlfriend or her sorority sisters or even where I'd find my next Kleenex. Everything that had happened seemed a little less serious. I felt a little less alone.

Now, I'd love to tell you that I got back to campus and all was right. That I immediately moved forward: Oprah's first success story. I'd love to tell you that, but I'd be lying. The rest of that winter was horrible for me. I saw the guy I'd been dumped for—did I mention that my girlfriend wasn't the most faithful?—riding around campus on the second-hand bike I'd bought, restored, and repainted for her as a Valentine's gift. I sat four rows behind them at a campus play, unable to hear the actors or get the knot out of my gut. I changed my routes to and from class, so that I would lessen the chances of seeing her.

And I obsessed. What had I done wrong? What did he have that I was missing? If I could just get her back, what changes could I make in myself so that I could keep her? The questions—and the hurt—took up the part of me that she'd once inhabited. I spent much of my time looking backward.

Until one afternoon that spring, when she asked if she could see me. We'd spoken a few times over the previous months, and even had a dinner. (Biggest waste of $12.95 for a steak ever, 'cause I couldn't eat one bite.) This time would be different; clearly she had something to say to me. I remember telling my roomies that I had no idea what she wanted, and I didn't even want to guess, but that was wrong. I wanted to guess that she wanted me back. I wanted that more than anything.

And you know what? She did. She wouldn't come out and say it, though. She wouldn't say, "Maybe we shouldn't have broken up; I'd like to try again." Instead, she started listing all the things her new boyfriend wasn't that I was.

Like considerate. And funny. And gentlemanly. And other good stuff. (How do I remember these things? I went home that night and wrote them down. Wouldn't you?)

She meant to compliment me, but she did it in such a back-handed way—comparing me to the guy she'd dumped me for and waiting for me to ask her for another chance—that I didn't react the way she expected I would. (Which was, roughly, "How could you have known he wasn't good enough for you? If you take me back, I think I could be! Please?") Nope. I got pissed. Not tearing-up-defenseless-teddy-bears pissed; I'd learned my lesson. Instead, I thanked her for telling me what she'd told me, and then I told her how insulting she was being. And then I left. No screaming, no witnesses, and best of all, no tears. Well, maybe she cried, but I sure didn't.

I was free.

Walking home that afternoon, I finally understood that I'd spent months looking in the wrong direction: backward. I was blaming myself for "losing" her. I was wondering about what I could do to get her back. And as much as it hurt, I was finding comfort in holding on to something that was gone, because at least I knew how I felt (lousy) and what I could expect. It was much safer than putting all those bad feelings aside and starting over.

The thought of starting over was *scary*. Would anyone else want me? How much rejection would I face . . . hell, how much could I *handle?* I realized on that walk back to my apartment that the thing I'd missed most about my girlfriend was having a fixed point in my life, the security of knowing whom I'd spend my Friday nights with. As long as I held on to the idea of winning her back—as long as I held on to my pain—I'd have a fixed point of a different sort. It would hurt, sure, but it would be less frightening than venturing out again into the unknown.

And then I realized something else. (This was an unusually productive walk.) Starting over meant having hope. Hope that someone *would* want me and would treat me with more respect than the person I'd just walked away from. Letting go of all the pain and embarrassment, of all of the "what if?" questions, meant I might actually be happy again. When I got home, I found the calendar that I used to keep track of all the movies I saw—I had a two-flick per week habit even then—and I opened it to the current week. There, on the right side of Thursday (and the left side of Friday) I drew a heavy vertical line.

I gave myself a stopper.

About six months later, I fell in love—with someone who didn't need to comparison shop before deciding I was worthy—for the first time.

I told you a few pages ago that I found three lessons in this whole Baloo-shredding, Oprah-watching tale of heartbreak. The first was about self-control, and how losing it can be more costly than you might think. The second lesson can be found in the title of this chapter: letting go. Holding on to things that aren't good for you—or, in my case, aren't even real—can be comforting, but happiness is never found when you're looking behind you. Learn whatever lessons you can from the things that happen to you, and then put those things aside, and look ahead. (In the Bible, God turns Lot's wife into a pillar of salt when she turns to take a last look back at her city, which God is in the process of destroying. That strikes me as excessive punishment but it makes the point: keep your eyes on what's ahead of you, and don't waste time on the bad things in your wake, because they have a way of sucking you back into them.)

The third lesson didn't hit me until about five years later, when I heard a song by a guy named Don Henley. It's a breakup song called "The Heart of the Matter," and though it pains me to admit that I had a major revelation thanks to something playing on Z-100, one line in that song hit me like a two-by-four. "I think it's about forgiveness," Henley sang, "even if you don't love me anymore." Now, you might think ol' Don was asking some woman to forgive him . . . but I don't. I don't think he meant her forgiveness at all.

Letting go *is* about forgiveness. It's about understanding all your own failings—the shame over making an ass of yourself, the weakness involved in wanting to run away—vowing to try to do better next time, and then letting yourself off the hook. Forgiving *yourself*.

One more quick stopper story, before we move on:

On the day I turned twenty-five, I gave myself another

stopper—this time because I was dating too much and couldn't seem to find anyone special. (I know, I know. It sounds like I'm bragging. But trust me: nothing is lonelier than spending a Saturday night with someone you're not interested in. You'll go on bad dates. You'll see.) I drew the line in the calendar and made myself a vow: no more dates for a while. I'd rededicate myself to my job and my friends, and stop trying so hard to fall in love.

The next day, I met my wife.

Long live the stopper.

CHAPTER EIGHT

TATTOOS

A guy says to his girlfriend, after they've been dating for five years, "Honey, I'm ready to take the plunge. I've found a great house for us, I've bought you a ring, and I'm getting down on my knee. Will you marry me?"

Through tears of joy, she says, "Of course! But I have one condition: I want you to tattoo my name on your shoulder first."

He hesitates. "Gosh, I don't know," he says. "A tattoo is so . . . *permanent.*"

It's an old joke but it makes a good point: tattoos are forever. If you ever seriously think about getting one, do yourself a favor first. Go to the drawer where you keep your T-shirts, and take a good look at them. What's on them? Got any designer names or funny sayings?

Or do you have T-shirts with pictures of cartoon animals? Wait, of course you don't: you had the animal T-shirts a few years ago, but you've gotten rid of them. You outgrew them . . . in a few different ways. Those worked just fine at a certain time in your life—when you were a little kid—but now you don't want the world to think you're immature, so you've cleaned your drawer out. Now maybe you've got Juicy Couture or Von Dutch, or whatever's considered cool this month.

Now go to where your Mom has her T-shirts, or check out a friend's mom's collection. Any Juicy shirts in there? Didn't think so. It's pretty pathetic when people over the age of thirty-five dress like they're teenagers. (Of course, if you *did* find Juicy shirts, your mother has my sincerest apology. And *you* have my complete sympathy.)

The point is that your look has changed, and it's going to change again. A hundred times. You'll cut your hair, or grow it. Maybe you'll dye it. You'll go through dozens of shades of nail polish and lipstick. The contents of your closet will change so often that you'll be convinced you're single-handedly keeping your local shopping mall in business. How you present yourself to the world is a fluid thing . . . it's rarely the same from one year to the next.

Now that you're done inspecting T-shirts, find your folks' high school yearbooks. For as geeky as they (and their friends) look to you in those pictures, their "looks" were perfectly acceptable when they were in school. They might not be caught dead in those wide lapels or shoulder pads today, and they wouldn't dream of having such big hair ever again, but at the time it was how people looked. You'll see your own school pictures years from now, and you'll barely recognize yourself.

See a pattern here? How we see ourselves changes, and fortunately we can keep up with that change. Clothes and hairstyles and makeup are all temporary, which is good because fashion is temporary, too. The human body—*your* body—is a work of art. But it's also your very own blank canvas, waiting for you, the artist, to give it color and style. If you look in a mirror and don't like what you see, you can peel away the makeup and clothes and start again.

When you decide to mark your body permanently, though, you're taking away a little bit of your ability to change. You're saddling yourself with a very specific look that you'll have to wear for the rest of your life, no matter how much your tastes or personality grow. You're quite literally branding yourself.

And "for the rest of your life" is a pretty long time, especially considering how much thought often goes into getting a tattoo. That is to say, not nearly enough. My friend Jim went to medical school with a guy who came back to the dorm one night with a brand new tattoo of a butterfly on his shoulder. When asked about it, he'd shake his head and say, "Never get drunk in Newport." (I would be willing to bet that if getting tattooed required passing a Breathalyzer test for alcohol, half the tattoo parlors in the world would go out of business.) Every time Jim's friend takes his shirt off, he's reminded of how dopey it can be to give in to impulse.

Don't get me wrong. I'm all for impulsive behavior when

it's over something small: reaching for someone's hand, ordering the double chocolate cake, buying a CD when you've only ever heard one song from it. It's a safe bet that you won't really regret those actions. Big things, though, life or body-altering things, should never be done on a whim. Or after cocktails. Big decisions deserve some thought.

And the bigger the decision, the more time you ought to think about it. In fact, I have a little trick that's always gotten me through the more important choices in my life, and it has to do with a "cooling off" period. Here's how it works:

When I'm faced with a big decision, the first thing I do is give myself a set period of time during which I *won't* decide anything. Could be hours, could be a few weeks. Depends on how important the decision is, you know? If I want to buy an expensive jacket, I make myself sleep on it. That keeps me from blowing the money and waking up mad at myself. If I walk out of the store, go home, and wake up still wanting the jacket, *then* I'm comfortable blowing the money.

Last time I looked for a car, I made myself wait one full week so that I'd have to shop around, and not let a car salesman catch me drooling over something impractical and talk me into it on the spot. When things got bad at a job I used to have, I gave the situation one month to improve. It didn't, and I was able to quit with a clear head . . .

and a well-thought-out plan for what I was going to do next. What I've found is that forcing myself to wait before making big decisions not only takes away the panic *before* I make them, it helps me feel more comfortable with them afterward.

Obviously, I hope you never decide to get tattooed. (I'd rather you stay away from body piercing, too, for the record. Tongue studs are just . . . *gross*.) If you do find yourself drawn to some kind of permanent marking, though, I'd suggest you force yourself to wait before making that choice. By my calculations, to properly evaluate the decision to get a tattoo would take . . . oh . . . twenty-five years or so.

It's hard to open a celebrity magazine these days without reading about stars who wish they'd thought just a little longer before making the decision to get a tattoo. In fact, read *People* or *Us* long enough, and you'll get to see both ends of the story: in one issue, the beautiful starlet is proudly displaying her husband's name in bold letters on her shoulder, and several issues later she's bad-mouthing her now ex-husband . . . and wearing sleeves.

A few years ago, a TV star's second husband had her portrait tattooed on his chest . . . and then appeared in some magazine a few years later, as part of a story on how difficult tattoo removal can be. (His next wife didn't like seeing her predecessor's face on her husband's flesh, I guess.)

When Johnny Depp stopped dating Winona Ryder, he had his "Winona Forever" tattoo changed to read "Wino Forever." It's a mildly funny solution to his problem, but you've got to figure that Johnny isn't really thrilled about sporting a tattoo that says he's an alcoholic. I bet he'd rather not have had that tattoo done in the first place.

I bet he wishes he'd done what my friend Dana does. She's the queen of temporary tattoos. She's had henna tattoos, hand-drawn ink temporaries, and even the kind that you press against your skin with a wet sponge. She's had religious tattoos, patterns that she's designed herself, cartoon characters, and even a few joke tattoos—those last ones usually for her husband's benefit.

Dana discovered temporary tattoos after her older sister went through the painful process of trying to remove a design she'd had tattooed around her upper arm. "She got it to upset our mom," Dana told me. "She wanted to 'get' her for being such a prude. But the only person she 'got' was herself, because after that she was always self-conscious without sleeves. On the beach, there was her tattoo. At a formal, there was her tattoo. At work . . ." You get the picture.

Dana, who had been thinking pretty seriously about a tattoo of her own, decided to try temporaries first, to make sure she liked whatever she ultimately chose well enough to look at it forever. What she found is that she liked variety. Some events called for fun tattoos; others for no tattoo at all. And the best part? "By the time I get bored with looking at a new tattoo," she said, "it's just about faded away."

Leaving her the chance to try something new and different, something that will match her latest style.

CHAPTER NINE

THE INTERNET

For most things you do, there's some kind of guidebook. Sports come with rules; gadgets come with instructions. Even proper letter writing is taught: the date goes at the top, followed by the address, and so on, all the way down to the "P.S." There are whole books written on what they call etiquette, which cover how to behave in any social situation. (These books come in handy when you're going to a fancy dinner party; they'll keep you from using your dessertspoon in your soup.) In other words, if you want to do something properly, there's usually a way to find out how.

The Internet—surfing, chatting, e-mailing—doesn't really have instructions, though. It's too new. Think of it this way: if the Internet were a person, it would still be in elementary school. So you can't even necessarily count on your parents to help you sort out sticky online situations, because we have about as much experience with this stuff as you do. Maybe less. The ability to instantly reach people, or to simultaneously "chat" with dozens of folks around the world is new to us, too, and chances are good we're making the same mistakes you are.

In fact, the Internet is so new, relatively speaking, that when my friend Gary called me at work one day in 1994 and said, "Dude, you gotta grab some domains," I had to ask him what the hell he was talking about. Did he expect me to buy houses, on my salary? Turns out he was telling me to take common words, add a ".com" to the end, and register them for myself. Like golf.com, or cars.com. There was this new thing called the World Wide Web, he said, and I could own some names that would be pretty valuable one day. Names I could sell to companies who would use them for something Gary called "websites." I wouldn't even have to pay anything; all I had to do was sign up for them.

Here was a guy with honest-to-God vision on the phone, handing me the key to untold wealth, and what did I do? I told him he was crazy, hung up, and went back to typing press releases. Gary, who registered a bunch of names and even started successful websites like match.com, is now a multimillionaire. Me, I'm still typing.

Still, I was curious about all this computer stuff, so when I found out about America Online later that year, I signed up. Pretty soon I was e-mailing, instant messaging, going into chat rooms, and yeah, I was even checking out websites. (And pounding my head against the wall because I hadn't listened to Gary when there was still time to register valuable names.) I was just about the first person among my friends—well, excluding Gary—to do any of this stuff.

Since AOL was just catching on, and public chat rooms weren't yet filled with creepy people, it was possible to actually find places to talk about your interests and make friends who shared them. I hung out in a chat room called the Writer's Café, where I chatted with everyone from a guy who's always on the bestseller list to a romance novelist I'm still friends with. We traded advice on dealing with agents and meeting deadlines, we gossiped, we talked about our marriages (or boyfriends or girlfriends), and we told gross jokes. Oh, and we all took turns caring for Lauren.

Lauren was a cancer patient living in a hospital in Texas. She was another regular in the Writer's Café, and she was online an awful lot. What else did she have to do, aside from getting radiation treatments and watching television? She'd send us her poetry, e-mail us about her loneliness, and from time to time she'd call one of us on the phone, and talk in her small voice about how much she wished her hair would grow back or her dad come visit her. (Her mom came every day, but her dad couldn't handle her illness, so he never went to the hospital.)

Lauren would never give any of us her address, because she didn't want us sending her presents or money, out of pity. Just being there for her in the chat room or on the phone was enough, she said. Still, we tried to do things for her. The bestselling author winked at the camera while on a morning news show, as a signal to her that he was think-

97

ing of her. Tanya, the romance novelist, tried to figure out which hospital Lauren was in, so she could plan a surprise visit. Lauren found out about Tanya's plans from someone else in the chat room, and firmly told Tanya to respect her privacy.

Not long after that, I got an IM from Tanya. "You're going to have to sit down for this one," she wrote, and being goofy, I typed back, *Duh*. I'm at my computer. You think I'm standing?" There was a pause. "Lauren's a fake," she typed.

Turns out Lauren wasn't sick, wasn't as young as she claimed, and wasn't even living in Texas. I don't remember anymore how Tanya finally found all this out, but I remember how sick I felt when she told me. This girl had made me care for her—had made all of us care for her—but she was playing an elaborate (and pretty twisted) game. Lauren sent one final e-mail to her friends in the Writer's Café, with a long and senseless explanation of why she'd fooled us all. She didn't even apologize. Then she disappeared.

But you know what? I bet she didn't disappear. I bet she just changed her screen name, came into our chat room as someone else, and got her jollies reading our chat about how much she'd fooled us. In fact, I suspected that right away, and I got so creeped out that I stopped going into the Writer's Café.

In the months that followed, I found dozens of similar stories in different chat rooms. People claimed to be one thing and turned out to be another. Usually they'd lie about how they looked or what kind of job they had. Mostly they'd do it to impress people or to try to get dates.

Faking people out is really easy on the Internet. When you're online, all anyone knows of you are words on a screen. They don't see your face, they can't hear your voice, they can't tell your age, sex, location, or anything else about you. The Internet is one big honor system . . . where you'll find out a lot of people aren't that honorable. Think you're talking to a cute fifteen-year-old boy from the high school in the next town? Surprise! He's really a fifty-year-old freak who wants you to meet him at the mall. That young cancer patient in Texas? She's an attention-starved housewife from Montana. There are all kinds of ways to fool folks . . . and if somebody gets caught in a lie online, they can just change their screen name and pretend to be someone else.

That's an easy thing to do, because people online are anonymous; you have no way of being sure of who they really are. Anonymity is what gives people the courage to make prank phone calls and send unsigned letters. The fact that they probably won't be caught helps them do things they would never own up to, you know? Sometimes those things are well-intentioned, like an anonymous note to warn a friend that she's got scary breath. Other times—most times—things are done anonymously because they're cruel, like scratching a nasty name onto some guy's locker when no one's around.

Anonymous things done online can be especially awful, because the Internet is a great way to spread horrible rumors at lightning speed. My friend has a daughter in seventh grade, and when her middle school set up a bulletin board on its website, it was promptly filled with gross (and untrue) stories about a certain girl having sex with a teacher in the school bathroom. When my friend's daughter posted something in defense of the girl, she was quickly called a "lying slut" on the board. Hundreds of people saw those posts, and my friend threatened to sue the school if they didn't drop their online bulletin board.

What really freaks parents out about the Internet, though, is that anonymous people—strangers—have such easy access to our kids. *In our own homes.* Think about it. If some random person you'd never met called on the phone and started trying to talk to you about school or your friends or what you like to do, you'd hang up on them fast. But if that same person found their way into a chat room you were in, and responded to things you were saying to friends, you might very well start talking to them, because that's what people do in chat rooms. Next thing you know, you're instant-messaging with them. If they seem fun or nice, you could start to trust them and the things they tell you about themselves . . . and maybe you'd start telling them things about you. Maybe—and this is what keeps your parents awake at night—you might decide there wouldn't be any harm in meeting them.

If you do any of that stuff with someone you know only

from a chat room, it means you've forgotten one of the first and most important things your folks ever taught you: don't talk to strangers.

Of course, even talking to people you *know* can be tricky online. You've already seen this stuff happen: friends who get annoyed if you don't respond to them quickly enough, or if they think you're instant-messaging someone else instead of them. Thanks to Buddy List boxes, it's harder and harder to have time to yourself online, or to hide from people you don't want to deal with. I know, I know; you can block certain people from seeing when you're signed on. That works as long as they don't find out you're chatting with someone else and realize you've blocked them. Then you're *really* in trouble.

My daughter Anna struggles with how to avoid certain people when she's online. She's got this one girl in her class, Janey, who always has to have a victim to torture so she can create a little drama. (You know the drill: Janey picks on a girl mercilessly until the girl turns around and yells at her, and then Janey cries, "You're so mean to me!" and her little group of followers all back her up. Anna's probably the fifth girl to be in Janey's gun sights this year alone.)

Anyway, in a pretty typical Janey kind of episode, Anna comes home from a movie one night, signs on to check her e-mail, and immediately gets an instant message from the witch: "Eww." Anna makes mistake #1: she answers. "What?" she types. "I said ewwww. It's u." comes Janey's reply, followed by "I'm with friends . . . let's see . . . 10 right now. At a party u weren't invited to." Neat kid, huh? It gets worse. Anna makes mistake #2: she tries to use logic to shut Janey up. "I don't remember starting a convo . . . and you don't want to talk to me . . . so I won't be hurt if you GO AWAY," she types.

It goes on this way for a few more lines. I walk into the room just as Janey tells Anna that she's "retarded & uglee." (Funny how often bullies are lousy spellers.) Anna asks me to remind her how to block people online . . . but she still seems bummed out after she blocks Janey. "What's the problem?" I ask, and Anna replies, "She'll just make up a new screen name and start all over. Am I supposed to block *everybody*?"

Not such an unusual story—pathetic bully taunts undeserving victim—except that it happened to Anna in her own room at 9:30 on a Friday night.

Now, if Janey got called on that stuff—on taunting classmates via instant messages—I don't doubt that she'd defend herself the way bullies always do: "I was *kidding*. Can't you take a joke?" Aside from the fact it would be a total lie, that would still be a pretty good defense, because of the one major problem with online chatting: it's hard to really communicate when all you have are words on a screen.

Think about how you talk to friends. You use facial expressions; you use your hands; you use your voice. All of these things clue your listener in to what you're really saying. You can give the same word about twenty different meanings depending on how you tilt your head or change your tone. (When we were kids, my sister Tesa could say the word "fine" in a way that made my blood run cold.) Most of the time, the words that we say to each other aren't quite as important as the way we say them.

It's hard to be sarcastic when you're typing, though. Or pensive. Or soothing. So it's easy to hurt people's feelings—whether you mean to or not—because you can't count on them to know how you mean what you type.

E-mailing can be even more treacherous than chatting; there are a hundred ways to mess up when you're sending notes online. Just ask the guy I know who wrote a really funny, really nasty poem about his boss—the first line was "Most half-wits have more wits than poor Marty Gorwitz" —and sent it to everyone on his mailing list. Too bad he'd forgotten that Marty's best friend was on his mailing list. He's got a different boss, now . . . and he never writes nasty poems on his computer anymore.

Or ask *me*: I once got such a poorly written e-mail from my friend Bob—he'd even signed off "wish you were *her*"—that I pointed out all his mistakes and added some funny comments, meaning to forward the e-mail to a mutual friend. Only I hit "reply" instead of "forward" and sent it right back to Bob. Fortunately, he had a sense of humor . . . and not a sharp knife.

Since the Internet is still so new—we're all still taking baby steps on the information superhighway—maybe the best advice for protecting ourselves online is the same stuff our parents told us when we were little:

Don't Talk to Strangers. A few pages ago, I mentioned this in regard to people in chat rooms, but they're not the only strangers you have to look out for online. Be very careful about websites that ask you for private information, like your name, address, and phone number. Usually they ask for that stuff so they can sell it to marketers: that's how your e-mail inbox gets clogged up with spam, how your snail-mail box gets jammed with junk mail, and it's how people who call up trying to sell you stuff get your number. I say "usually" because there are also far more sinister uses for that kind of information, uses I don't want to describe and you don't want to think about. So keep your private stuff private.

Similarly, *Don't Take Candy From Strangers.* It's scary how often e-mail attachments turn out to carry viruses that can destroy your computer. Never download anything unless you know who sent it to you, and even then, it's a good idea to ask them what it is before you open it. Some of the nastiest computer viruses are able to use the e-mail address books of infected computers and send *themselves* around. So you think you're getting some funny JPEG from a friend, when instead you're getting a destructive piece of computer code created by some hacker in Berlin. I speak from experience. I have the tech support bills to prove it.

Play Nice. Be really careful not to write unkind things in e-mails or instant messages unless you're ready for everyone you know to read them—because everyone you know just might.

Take It Slow. The best advice in life just keeps coming back. Not too long ago, I bought my first boat. The guy who sold it to me could tell I was intimidated—I'd never driven one before—so he gave me a great piece of advice: go slow, get into trouble slow. His point was that I couldn't do much damage to my boat—or to anyone on it—if I used basic caution. If I didn't drive really fast in waters I wasn't too familiar with. If I took the time to practice basic stuff like pulling in and out of the slip. Moving slowly isn't always much fun, but it sure beats wrecking the boat or injuring someone because I'm moving faster than I'm comfortable with.

That's great advice when it comes to navigating the Internet. The second you're unsure how to deal with a person in a chat room, or how to respond to an IM, slow down. Give yourself time to think. Sign off, even . . . it's hard to get into too much trouble for the stuff you *don't* type.

Oh, and one more piece of Internet guidance, before we move on. If my friend Gary calls, and offers you any business advice? *Listen to him.*

CHAPTER TEN

GRIEF

John Cosgrove was legendary among the kids at Middlesex Junior High for the pranks he'd play on teachers. This one time, John walked up to Mr. Trinkaus, our eighth grade science teacher, and moved his lips as if he were asking a question, but made no sound. Mr. Trinkaus wore an old-fashioned hearing aid, and he assumed he couldn't hear John because it was set too low. So he said, "Wait a moment, son," turned up the dial, and John again moved his lips, this time letting out a slight whisper. Mr. Trinkaus cranked up the volume on his hearing aid even higher, and then John screamed "MR. TRINKAUS, I JUST WANTED TO ASK YOU . . ." We basically had to pull the poor old guy off the ceiling, he jumped so high.

I was John's lab partner in science, and I sat with him in Mr. Klein's social studies class, too, as well as a few others. Along with my best friend Jim Cleaver, John and I managed the basketball team. I saw an awful lot of him every day.

And then one day I didn't, because he died.

107

I sat next to empty chairs for a few weeks, and could feel the stares of the kids who'd barely known John and wondered what I knew about his death. We all had some vague understanding that he'd had an accident at home, and before long there were crazy stories going around. He'd been trying out a magic trick that had gone wrong, someone said to Jimmy. He must have been unhappy and killed himself, I was told over lunch. The kid who said that was bigger than me, and swatted me away pretty easily when I took a swing at him. A girl whose mom was friends with a woman who once lived near the Cosgroves solemnly told our math class that she heard John was murdered.

The rumors eventually died down, seating assignments got changed so that I didn't have to sit next to any more empty chairs, and most of the kids at Middlesex forgot about John. Except me. I couldn't. But where I'd been encouraged to talk about him by everyone for the first few weeks, suddenly it was clear that any mention of him made other kids uncomfortable. In the span of one month, the subject of John's death went from unavoidable to unmentionable. "Get over it" seemed to be the big theme whenever I tried to talk about it.

So I found someone who *had* to listen. I went to a priest from my church. I told him about how much I hurt; how even watching certain TV shows made me sad because John and I used to talk about them; and how I felt changed in a way that made people not want to hang around with me. In response, the priest said, "We can't know why God would take someone so young. We have to have faith that God has a plan, and that John has gone to be with his heavenly Father."

Though I was asking how to cope with what had happened, the priest wanted to answer a different question: he wanted to explain *why* it had happened. I went home feeling even worse than before I'd gone to the church. It hadn't even occurred to me that God had "taken" John, but now I started to think about that, too. Why would God want to pull a kid away from his family and friends?

Grief is a two-headed monster. When someone you love dies, you feel the pain of losing them along with confusion over why they're gone. Either one of those feelings would be plenty to deal with on its own; put loss and confusion together and the whole thing can feel almost overwhelming. So most people look for answers, thinking that if they can only understand why someone has died, it would make the sense of loss a little easier to bear.

That's exactly what I did some years after John's death, when my friend Heidi Craig flipped her car over while coming home from a summer job. She died a few days later. Heidi and I had gone to high school together, and we went to colleges just a few hours away from each other in the Midwest. When I hit a rough patch freshman year, it was Heidi who got in her car and came to visit; when her love life had her in knots—which was often—it was my phone she rang for advice. I loved her dearly, from her goofy laugh to her beautiful eyes to her giant heart. All of which was taken away late on a weekday afternoon, in a one-car accident on I-95.

What sense did that make? What would God need with a college student? I went looking for answers. A minister in town told me roughly the same thing my priest had said years before: "We can't fully understand *blah blah blah* . . . God has a plan *blah blah blah* . . ." I went back to school that fall feeling a little more alone and just as confused about "God's plan" as ever. The fact that Heidi had died for no other reason than she hadn't bothered putting on her seatbelt gnawed at me. Was God punishing her carelessness, or did God make sure she didn't buckle up because it was her time?

Heidi's death seemed so absurd . . . that it started to make sense. I began to think about how silly it is to believe that there is some set time and date for each of us to die. If that were the case, why bother wearing seatbelts? Or going to the doctor? Or putting guard rails on mountain highways? I mean, if God's plan says it's time for you to go, then it's time for you to go, right?

What a sad, pointless world this would be if that were true, I realized. Heidi died because we all die: life is fragile. Whether it's old age, sickness, a natural disaster, or a silly, avoidable accident on the highway, something is going to happen to each of us that will end our time on earth. There's an old saying that the only two things we can be certain of in life are death and taxes, but that's wrong: I've known a few folks who've never paid taxes. We all die, though, rich or poor, famous or anonymous.

Which means that God doesn't need to "take" us, because death is unavoidable. It's part of the package. In a funny way, that's what makes life so beautiful. You don't know how long you have on earth, so you need to get in as much *living* as you can while you're here. Putting things off, waiting for "some other time" isn't terribly wise when now might be all you have. Think of it this way: Isn't each day of summer vacation sweeter because you know school is going to come around again in the fall? Wasn't the ball Cinderella crashed with the help of her fairy godmother that much more magnificent because she had to hightail it out of there by the stroke of midnight? Life is beautiful *because* of its fragility, because of the urgency with which we ought to live it.

Once I got rid of the notion that God sits up in heaven with this big calendar, "taking" people on their preassigned days, I lost the confusion that made my sadness over Heidi seem overwhelming. Which left me with the sadness. And that was plenty, *thankyouverymuch*.

For months, I got sucker-punched by loss and sorrow. Turning the pages of my address book, I'd glimpse her name and number, and find myself afraid to look at it. I couldn't cross it out—how weird would that be?—but seeing it was terrible. Someone else would answer that phone now, just as someone else was living in her old room at school. It felt like Heidi had been erased. Going to the

Water Tower Mall in Chicago was hard, too, because it reminded me of Heidi's disastrous attempt to help me dress better. How I bribed her with chocolate mints from Marshall Field's to get her to shop with me. How she rolled her eyes when I showed her the cowboy boots I wanted to buy. How she made the "I'm gonna throw up" sign when I pulled a pastel-colored jacket off the rack. (It was the 1980s. You have no idea how lucky you are to have missed the 1980s.) It seemed that just about anything could bring Heidi to mind . . . and of course nothing could bring her back.

I felt so lonely. When my friend Katie Couric lost her husband a few years back, she told me that one of the hardest things about losing someone you love is that the rest of the world goes on. Here you are, filled with grief, wondering how you'll move forward, but everywhere you turn people are talking and laughing and arguing and doing all the things normal people do. How can they not see that the world has changed? At exactly the time you need other people the most, you end up feeling cut off from them, separated by a sadness you know they can't really understand.

After a little while has passed, you'll notice that people around you are made uncomfortable by your grief. Want to know why that is? It's because of television. I'm not completely kidding.

Thanks to thousands of hours spent watching sitcoms and family dramas, we've become addicted to the notion that every problem in life can be solved by the final commercial break. Some boy is experimenting with booze? Oh, something terrible will *almost* happen, and it will scare him into staying away from the bottle. His parents will ground him . . . and then hug him tight as the episode ends. A girl vandalizes her school along with her friends? She'll feel guilty, then tearfully confess and get an after-school job to pay off the damages. Then—lesson learned—Mom and Dad will hug her in time for the fade-out.

When someone you love dies, there aren't any easy lessons for you to digest; there's no "Gosh, I've overcome that obstacle!" moment. Grief can't be "fixed." It has to be endured, and it can take a long, long time to feel manageable. That's a hard thing for most people to face, especially when there are a million self-help books telling them they can achieve anything as long as they work hard enough. My friend Liz Auran, who encouraged me to write this book partly because she lost her dad as a young woman, says that his death was the first thing she ever faced that couldn't be resolved or neatly tied up or "finished." Though he's been dead for some twenty years now, Liz still feels the dull ache of missing him. Time has lessened it, but it's there.

When grief finds you, you have to live through it; but that doesn't mean there's nothing you can do to make it a little more bearable. First off, forgive the people who seem uncomfortable with your sadness. That's their problem, not yours. Keep talking about how you feel, because the folks that love you will find that they can handle it, and the ones that can't . . . well, you're better off without them. People who love you *want* to help you, but sometimes their fear that they don't know how comes off looking like annoyance that you're asking for help. When they realize that just being there for you—just listening to you even when they don't know what to say—is all you're asking of them, they'll be able to give you what you need.

Second, force yourself to live your life. Go out and do things. That will be incredibly hard, because part of you will feel like it's a betrayal of the person you've lost. Part of you will be convinced that the way to honor someone's memory is to lock yourself away and grieve. That part of you will be wrong. When you move forward with your life, it's not a way of forgetting someone—as if!—but instead, it's a way of honoring them. It's a way of saying that all the feelings and memories that grief has left you with are an important part of who you are.

Locking yourself away in a dark room and waiting for the pain of loss to go away might seem easier on you, at first. But what happens over time is that you start equating that lonely, dark room with any thoughts you might have of the person you lost. Memories = locking yourself away = pain. When you make the effort to carry on, or to go to school or your job or out with friends, the pain will lessen a little faster, and those memories will become a natural, welcome part of your life. You'll be carrying the person you loved with you, forever.

Though it doesn't happen often anymore, memories of

my friend John Cosgrove still stop by to say hello at the oddest moments. Sometimes it happens when a little blond kid with an angelic face but a devilish attitude crosses my path, and sometimes it's when somebody pulls off a great practical joke. John would have appreciated that, I think, and it makes me happy. I still think of Heidi Craig all the time. So much of what I know about girls came from endless long-distance phone calls with her, and so many of my best high school memories have her in them.

See, that's what happens when time has taken away some of the sting of grief. As the hurt and sadness slowly recede, what's left behind are memories and a feeling of incredible gratitude: yes, I miss my friends, but I am so lucky to have had them in my life, for however brief a time they were here. Missing them helps me to understand the fragility of life, and to be grateful for the wonderful friends who are still with me.

CHAPTER ELEVEN

SELF-CONTROL

So I had this weird problem with my jaw, and the doctor told me the only way to fix it was for him to sort of pop it back into place. Sounds fun, right? I was more than a little freaked. Relax, the doctor told me, this is a common procedure, and we'll give you this stuff so you'll be awake, but not really . . . and you won't feel a thing.

He was right. They put a needle in my arm, I got drowsy, and that's all I remember.

Which is why it bugged me for days that the nurses and staff in that doctor's office smiled at me so strangely when I left that afternoon, and seemed to nudge each other and giggle when I came back for a follow-up visit. Clearly, I said or did something really embarrassing while I was drugged up and woozy, but I have no idea what it was. I don't know why they were all laughing. I *do* know I'm never going back to that doctor again.

People who lose control of themselves are funny; that's why we see so many drunk or stoned characters in come-

117

dies. They act like fools, and we laugh. They say stupid things, and we laugh. They fall down, throw up, and pass out, and we keep on laughing.

Remember that when one of your friends pushes you to get drunk at a party. Could be that they think getting wasted will help you have a good time . . . then again, could be they're hoping that you'll be the entertainment. That *you'll* be the one saying stupid things, falling down, or passing out. You'll be the one that people laugh at.

The thing is, getting laughed at is the least of your worries when you make the decision to give up your self-control. And that's exactly what drugs and alcohol take from you: your ability to control your own actions. To know what you're saying and doing.

Quick: what's one of the hardest things about being a teenager? Convincing your parents that you know what's best for you, that you have good judgment. You've got the whole crossing-the-street thing down; you've mastered the not-talking-to-strangers bit. You'll even, some of the time, get yourself to bed at a reasonable hour when you've got a test the next day. So why can't we trust you to go to parties, and to maybe have a beer or two?

Because the whole point of drinking or doing drugs is to make you lose *that judgment.* See the problem? We know that you're smart and that you've learned a lot about how to protect yourself. We also know that one of the ways you learn things is by trying and failing. If you make mistakes while learning how to cook, the worst thing that happens is you make a mess of the kitchen. But if you screw up while you're drunk or stoned . . . lives can get ruined. We freak over the idea of your using booze and drugs because there's not much margin for error there.

The Randall kids were all really well-liked. Tommy Randall, the third born, was nineteen and a jock in his freshman year at Boston University. He was a genuinely nice guy and a hell of a lot of fun to be around because he could talk to anyone about anything. And Tommy was the peacekeeper: if someone stepped out of line with his friends, he'd jump right in and straighten them out—as politely as he could—before things got ugly. His level head served him really well on the playing field, where he earned himself a scholarship; and in the bars on Cape Cod, where he stopped a lot of fights. Tommy could drink with the best of them, and in the early summers, before he'd have to get ready for football season, that's just what he did.

So one July night he's taking the back roads, heading to a party from a bar in town, when he loses control of his family's Chevy station wagon. Since he's had about seven tequila shots on top of a few beers, he has no idea why this is happening, nor will he be able to explain it to the cops later, when they ask him how he ended up spinning into a telephone pole, wrecking the car.

You thought I was going to tell you Tommy died. He didn't. Walked away without a scratch, actually. So did three of the four passengers in the car. Not a serious injury among them. The fourth passenger was Tommy's sister Beth. She was thrown twenty-five feet from the car. *She* died.

Beth had been eighteen for all of four months and was getting ready to go to Yale, also on an athletic scholarship. She taught swimming to make money for school, and on the side she was a lifeguard at a local country club. The guys all loved her—though respectfully, considering Tommy and her other (equally large) brothers—and the girls wanted to be her. Her father liked to joke that she was the first cheerleader ever to get into an Ivy League college.

Among the photos on the Randall mantle was an eight-by-ten of Beth, in her cheerleading outfit, standing with her arm around big brother Tommy in his grass-stained football uniform. In it, her hand looks almost comically small on his shoulder pad. At the reception after the funeral, more than one person remarked on how unbearably sad that photo made them.

Tommy never went back to school and never forgave himself. Last anyone heard, he works construction, and he still drinks. A lot. Beth's friend Rachel was hit almost as hard: the night of the accident, Beth had offered to drive, but Rachel told her that Tommy was just fine and she shouldn't worry. She was sitting next to Beth when Beth was thrown out the window.

Most adults can tell you a similar story or two; every town has its tragic stories about kids who died too young because somebody drove drunk. Most adults—if they're honest—will also tell you that *they* did stupid things when they were drunk or stoned, like getting behind the wheel of a car or riding along even though they knew the driver was drunk. Like I said, they'll tell you if they're being honest.

But most adults *won't* be honest, and you can't really blame us. We worry that you'll hear our stories and you'll reason it this way: Mom and Dad just admitted that they got drunk a bunch of times and did things they weren't proud of . . . so they can't get mad at me for drinking or smoking pot or whatever, 'cause then they'd be hypocrites. We worry that if we're honest, you'll take it as a big green light to go out and do the same dumb things we did.

We're not so much worried that you'll show the same stupidity we did; we're afraid you won't have the same dumb luck that we had. We don't want *you* to be the story people tell their kids to convince them not to drink.

Somewhere between being laughed at and dying in a car wreck are the other dangers of drinking and drugs, the ones that you're much more likely to face. They're the things that cause the scars you *can't* see, the ones most people don't want to talk about.

Junior and senior years of high school, the best parties were at my friend Steve's. We all figured the FBI had his folks hidden away in the witness protection program because they were never around. His house was high school heaven: no parents, great stereo, lots of rooms, and a

121

kitchen table big enough for eight people to play this beer-drinking game you've never heard of called "quarters." Steve had only two rules on party nights: nobody changed the music but him—since he played almost nothing but Bruce Springsteen, that was fine by me—and people had to come in carpools with what we would eventually call a designated driver. Whoever drove couldn't drink. (One of the bigger jerks at Darien High School challenged Steve on that, and Steve argued it this way: "If some idiot wrecks his car, and the cops find out where he was, I'll never be able to have another party again." The jerk shut up. Hard to argue with logic.)

So this one night in May, just before the end of junior year, I get to Steve's house to find more cars than I've ever seen in his driveway. The quarters table is packed, and there are a good dozen people waiting to jump into the game. In the living room, there's a lot more drinking going on, and I immediately notice two strange things. First, there are three people that I know—and don't really like—dressed like they're mobsters out of the 1930s. Fedoras, pinstriped suits, wide ties, the whole thing. Only last I'd heard, this wasn't a costume party. They're sort of off by themselves, looking around the room and whispering to each other, like they've got some big inside joke.

The other thing I notice is Donna. I don't think I'd ever seen her at one of Steve's parties. She's always been shy and kind of serious. This isn't her crowd. And yet here she is . . . and she's talking to two pretty popular guys. You'd almost think they're fighting over her. I see one of them, Russell, hand her a refill on her drink. Looks like orange juice, so I'm guessing she's drinking a screwdriver, which is OJ mixed with vodka. Big Gulp-sized.

While Steve and I scream along with Bruce's "Rosalita," Donna goes upstairs with Russell. When they come back down a little while later, Russell heads into the kitchen to play quarters, and Brian, the other guy she'd been talking to earlier hands her another giant drink. She takes it, and the two-girls-and-a-guy playing dress-up start whispering to each other. One of them goes to the kitchen.

Here's what I find out about a half-hour later, after I see Donna being led back upstairs, this time by Brian:

The three mobsters aren't trying to be mobsters at all. They're dressed as old-time gamblers. The pieces of paper stuck into the brims of their hats are meant to look like betting slips from a racetrack. They've made this a theme party, and the theme is "the Donna Derby." How it works is simple. Russell and Brian are having a contest to see who can get the furthest with Donna sexually. They think this is a worthy challenge because Donna's not just a virgin, she's never gone past kissing anyone, and she's only done *that* a couple of times. Each wants to prove that he's the bigger stud.

(All of this has been dreamed up by Michelle, a friend of Russell's. She's one of the two girls wearing the gambler costumes, and she actually has money on Russell.)

The Donna Derby comes apart when the one guy

dressed up as a gambler comes back from the kitchen with news on what happened between Donna and Russell. He's holding up two fingers, like he's flashing the peace sign. "Second," he says, meaning second base. Russell told him he'd gotten his hand up her shirt, but she'd stopped him when he'd tried to unbutton her pants. Michelle and the other girl are laughing hysterically, and people around them start listening in, wondering what's going on. The three schemers decide it's time to let the party in on their game.

What they don't think about before proudly telling people what they're up to is that Steve, the host, is a good guy. He gets pissed off. He and his friend Paul go upstairs and bang on the door of the room where Donna has just gone with Brian. When Brian comes out, he's brought downstairs and shoved out the front door. Along with the "gamblers." Russell tells Steve to calm down, and that's when things *really* go bad.

Remember that a lot of the people involved are either drunk or well on their way. Tempers get lost, and a few punches get thrown. An antique wooden chair in the front hallway gets destroyed when Russell gets pushed and loses his balance.

Upstairs, Donna—drunker than everyone else combined thanks to her three vodka Big Gulps—starts sobbing when a couple of girls explain to her what's been going on. She pushes the girls out of the room and locks herself in.

It takes an hour, but Steve, Paul, and I get everyone

calmed down and out the door, except for the two girls trying to talk Donna out of the bedroom. While we're cleaning up, we hear her let them in. Then we hear some more crying, and eventually, some vomiting. Paul and I shoot fingers to see who's going to drive them all home. I lose.

Can you guess that this is the longest drive of my life? I spend most of it trying to think of something comforting to say, and the rest of it feeling tiny, because I can't.

It's often said of alcohol that it makes you "lose your inhibition." Inhibition is another way of saying self-restraint, so losing it means losing your ability to keep yourself from doing things. When people tell you to lose your inhibition, they think they're giving you good advice: *You're too uptight, and you need to loosen up. Have a drink.*

Well guess what? Inhibitions are your way of protecting yourself. Donna hadn't been intimate with anyone before that party; she was inhibited physically because she wasn't ready emotionally. Russell and Brian kept handing her drinks in the hopes that she would lose those inhibitions. And it worked: Russell "got to second base" with her, and Steve told me later that night that it looked like Brian was about to get a lot further when he busted in on them. (It's important to understand that Donna wasn't a completely helpless victim here: she made the very bad decision to drink herself senseless.)

Example #3,652 of how the world is biased against girls: if either Russell or Brian had been successful in having sexual intercourse with a very drunken Donna, *her* reputation would have been ruined . . . and theirs would have improved. Even though they used vodka to cloud her judgment. Even though neither of them was romantically interested in her, and she would have been a good and faithful girlfriend to either of them. They would have been called studs, and she would have been thought of as a drunken slut.

It's *because* the world is so unfair that you've got to be that much more careful than boys. And the best way to protect yourself is to keep your judgment sharp and to use it. If someone is pushing you to drink, think really hard about why it is they want you drunk.

If someone is pushing you to do drugs, don't think. Run. Run as far from them as you possibly can.

Drugs, like pot, cocaine, and ecstasy come with exactly the same problem as alcohol: they take away your judgment. Change the word "booze" to "drugs" in everything that I've told you so far, and the stories would remain the same. Drugs get people killed in stupid accidents, and drugs are used to get people to do things they might otherwise have the sense not to.

But drugs are a hundred times scarier than alcohol for two simple reasons: you run a real risk of becoming addicted, and you don't ever really know what it is you're taking.

Booze is sold in stores, and the government makes sure

that it is exactly what you think it is. Beer, wine, and liquor have to carry labels telling you not only their ingredients, but also what their exact alcohol content is. Drink a beer, and you know what to expect. Have a shot of tequila, and you know what to expect.

Good luck knowing what you're sticking up your nose when you snort coke. Think a drug dealer is going to supply you with a content label? For that matter, think he cares what happens to you, when you use what he sells you? Not likely. So maybe that bag of coke is fine . . . then again, maybe it has heroin in it . . . or another drug called PCP. And remember that drugs pass through a bunch of hands—one guy sells coke to another guy, who splits it up and sells it to three other guys, who split it up and sell it to people like *you*—so maybe someone added rat poison somewhere along the line, to make the bags fuller, so they could charge more for them.

My friend Will learned this the hard way in a club. His friends were all snorting coke, so he decided he'd give it a try. They thought it was funny, how he seemed to be confused right after he did it . . . how he didn't remember anyone's names . . . how he panicked. They thought it was less funny when he started scratching so hard at his own face that he bled. It wasn't funny at all when a security guy at the club called an ambulance.

The doctor told Will (the next day, when he no longer thought his brain was melting) that what he'd taken wasn't just cocaine, it was cocaine mixed with lysergic acid di-

127

ethylamide—better known as LSD or acid. Then the doctor offered to walk him down to the morgue, so he could see the sixteen-year-old girl who'd overdosed on the exact same mixture. "You're a very stupid young man," the doctor told him. "But a very lucky one."

I like what the doctor said to Will, because by mentioning luck, he points out that giving up your self-control to alcohol or drugs is a game of chance . . . where the stakes are awfully high. I haven't met anybody who thinks that they "won" when they got drunk or stoned, but I know a bunch who will tell you they lost. Giving up your self-control is a wager where there's no chance of winning . . . and you need a lot of luck to avoid losing. In Las Vegas, they have a name for that.

It's called a Sucker's Bet.

CHAPTER TWELVE

CYNICISM

Sugar Ray Leonard was one of the greatest fighters ever. He won an Olympic gold medal and went on to win championship belts in something like five different weight classes. The guy used to make his opponents crazy because he never stood still. He'd hit them, and then he'd be gone. Hit them and slide away. Hit them and dance out of reach. Though it sounds strange, watching him fight was one of the most beautiful things I've ever seen.

About four years after he won his gold medal, Ray fought Roberto Duran, a Panamanian fighter with no flash but plenty of power. If Ray Leonard had the style of a matador, Duran had the heart of the most ferocious bull. It was a match every boxing fan in the world wanted to see.

Especially me. I was really into boxing as a kid, mostly because watching fights on television was a way to spend time with my dad. Boxing gave us something to talk about that wasn't my schoolwork or his job. I would tell him what I'd read about a fighter in *The New York Times,* and he'd tell me about the fights he'd been to years before, and how fighting styles changed and changed back. We spent a lot of time predicting what would happen in each fight based on what we knew about the boxers.

On the morning of the Leonard-Duran fight, I gave my dad what I thought was a pretty easy prediction: Leonard was going to mop the floor with Duran. He'd dance around poor Roberto for a few rounds, tire him out, and then take him apart. The matador always beats the bull.

My dad shook his head. "Leonard's going to lose," he told me over his breakfast. I nearly choked on the Frosted Flakes I'd just shoveled into my mouth. I'm sure I looked at him as if he was insane.

"Here's what's going to happen," said my dad. "Leonard's going to go out and fight toe-to-toe against this guy. He's not going to dance, he's going to trade punch for punch. And he's going to lose by decision." (If neither fighter gets knocked out, the judges decide the winner based on points.)

I had no idea what to say. Clearly, my dad *was* deranged. "Philip," he said, his tone now kind of condescending, "That's what's going to happen, and here's why: Everybody expects Leonard to win. If he does, there's no reason for a rematch, and a rematch would mean a lot more money for both fighters. If Leonard *does* lose tonight, and then wins a rematch, there's even more money for a third fight. It's happened before. It's the game."

My dad went back to his paper, and I went back to my

cereal, dazed and a little angry. Ray Leonard was as close to a hero as I had. How could my dad believe he'd purposely lose?

And how could he seem so smug the next morning, when he turned out to be right about the outcome of the fight? As predicted, Ray Leonard tried to fight Duran straight on and lost by decision. I grabbed another section of the paper and pretended to read. I didn't want to talk about the fight. My father tried once or twice, I mumbled a few answers, and we dropped it.

Months later, on the day of the Leonard-Duran rematch, I'm sitting in the basement of my friend Steve's house watching television when the local sports guy comes on and starts talking about the fight. "Duran's gonna win again," Steve said. "The brawler always wins."

"Not a chance. Here's what's going to happen," I said, and then I launched into my father's explanation of why Leonard lost the first fight and was going to win tonight. I didn't give my dad credit, though. I made it sound like this was my own theory. Steve listened patiently, and then shook his head, saying, "Man, that's the most cynical thing I've ever heard."

Leonard won the fight. In fact, he was delivering such a beating that in the middle of a round Duran just walked away, saying, "No more" in Spanish as he went back to his corner. I nodded knowingly at Steve the next day, as if to say, "See? It's all a big fraud." He didn't want to talk about it—kind of like me, the morning after the first fight. I'd ruined boxing for him, just like my dad had ruined it for me.

Cynicism is a belief in . . . nothing. You've already met cynics, I'm sure: they're those people who tell you they see things how they *really* are, and that things are really rotten. They believe that no one is sincere, and that everyone has secret, selfish reasons for the things they do. They'll tell you that everything is rigged against you, and no one means what they say. The world, according to the cynic, is a cold and cruel place.

And that last part is true—for the cynic. People who are cynical, or jaded, *make* their own lives cold because they lack courage. It takes courage to believe in things; sometimes things *will* disappoint you, sometimes people will let you down. To have faith is to risk having your heart broken, and the cynic isn't willing to take that risk.

I look at cynics and I think it must be very tiring, being so world-weary. They have to practice their sneers and their deep sighs, constantly update their all-black wardrobes, and keep searching for new synonyms for "fraud" and "phony." It must be hard, believing the worst about everything and everyone. It must be hard, being so joyless.

See, that's the price that cynics pay: they never get to feel joy. Sure, they never feel pangs of disappointment, but when things work out for them, when something good happens, they don't get to celebrate, because that would mean admitting they're wrong. In order to protect themselves from disappointment, they deny themselves satisfaction.

The older you get, the more you'll see what a cynical world you live in. You might get interested in politics, only to have people around you dismiss your interest with a quick "Oh, all politicians are liars." You might decide to study law, only to hear how all lawyers are greedy people with no interest in what's right or wrong. You might—strike that: you *will*—fall in love, only to be told by your friends that you better know how to "play the game."

In fact, the most cynical book I've ever seen is on that very subject. It's an advice book for women on how to get a man and keep him . . . all by playing according to "the rules." (That's actually the title: *The Rules*.) Don't talk to a new boyfriend on the phone for too long, says the book, and always be the one to end the conversation. If he calls you on Thursday to ask you out for Saturday night, pretend you already have plans, so you don't seem too available. Stuff like that. *The Rules* was a huge bestseller and spawned a bunch of sequels written by the same authors. One of them is called *The Rules of Marriage: Time Tested Secrets for Making Your Marriage Work,* which is kind of funny when you consider that one of the co-authors of the *Rules* books got divorced just after that one came out.

Actually, that's not funny—it's kind of sad. I'm sorry that the author's marriage didn't work, but then again I can't say I'm surprised. *The Rules* tell you to lie and manipulate in order to find a partner . . . but common sense tells you that any relationship based on lies and manipulation isn't going to be very strong. In fact, it's not even a relationship, if you want to get technical about it: if you have to "play" by the "rules," it's a *game*.

A quick test, to see if you're already a cynic: Re-read those last two paragraphs. If your reaction is "See? Even the woman who wrote the book on how to 'make your marriage work' got divorced, so marriage is impossible," you're in big trouble. You're *way* too young to be so jaded. Lighten up, okay?

I suspect you didn't say that, though. You've seen—and you know—what the cynic has either forgotten or refuses to see: most people are pretty decent. Though I fail from time to time, I know that I try to be. Don't you? So if everyone is selfish and awful, like cynics believe, shouldn't you and I be selfish and awful, too?

When someone I know says something cynical that begins with either "everyone" or "everything," I like to challenge them. For instance, I used to work with a woman named Diane, who'd had a bad string of relationships and decided that all men are liars. We knew each other pretty well, so I asked her if she thought *I* was a liar. "Well, no," she said, "but that just makes you the exception that proves the rule, you know?" No, I told her, I didn't know: "What about your dad?" Okay, Diane said, he wasn't a liar either. We went down a long list of men who weren't liars until she threw up her hands, frustrated with me. "Alright already!" she cried. "Fine. All men are *not* liars." I smiled in a kind of 'see? I told you so' way. She punched me in the arm. "But you're all obnoxious," she added.

For Diane, it was much easier to believe that "all guys are liars," because it kept her from having to really look at herself. (Being a cynic means that nothing is ever *your* fault: the world is stacked against you, so you're blameless.) When she eventually gave it some hard thought, she realized that her lousy love life was due to her lousy choices. Great looks and hot cars belonged a little lower on her list of reasons to date a guy, she decided. "Maybe manners are more important than a Porsche," is how she put it to me.

Once she understood what the *real* problem was, Diane stopped using sentences that began "All guys are . . ." (Though she may still believe we're all obnoxious. And she just might be right about that one.) The point is that once she used her head, she stopped being cynical.

The tricky thing about cynicism is that it's so common, you don't always know you're feeling it, and so it's not always easy to fight.

My friend Bernie Katz is a big opera buff. Not too long ago, he had the chance to see the farewell performance of Luciano Pavarotti, probably the greatest—and certainly the most famous—opera singer in the world. If you want to know how excited Bernie was, think about your favorite singer, imagine you've been listening to him or her for decades, and now imagine you've got a chance to see their very last concert. (If Elvis Costello or Bruce Springsteen announces a farewell tour, I'm going to be at every show. Early. Wearing the T-shirt.)

Bernie was pretty excited. He went off to the Metropolitan Opera House in New York's Lincoln Center, took his seat, and immediately found out he'd been wrong to leave his camera at home. The Met, usually very strict about its "no pictures" policy, had realized what a big night this was, and was letting fans take pictures throughout the show. Most of the other concertgoers seemed to have cameras. Bernie was bummed.

During an intermission, it struck him that he could ask the man in the seat next to him if he'd mind sharing a picture or two; Bernie would gladly pay to have something to remember the evening by. Bernie told his wife that when the man came back to his seat, he was going to ask him.

Bernie's wife reacted exactly the way most of us would. "Are you crazy?" she said. "He's a total stranger. Why would he go to the trouble for you?" Bernie had to admit he was wondering the same thing. Still, he politely handed the guy his card and made his request. The guy seemed embarrassed by the question, put Bernie's card in his pocket, and turned his attention back to the concert.

Hey, Bernie told himself, at least I tried.

Two weeks later, Bernie got an envelope in the mail: a few snapshots of Pavarotti on stage and a lovely note were inside. The guy didn't even want Bernie to pay for the prints.

Mrs. Katz isn't a cynic, but she had the same cynical reaction most of us would have had when faced with Bernie's decision to ask a stranger for a favor. Why would someone he'd never met want to help him? Bernie fought his own cynicism, and got not only some pictures of Pavarotti's farewell but also some proof that people can be pretty swell, if you give them a chance.

I don't really think my dad is a cynic either, though for some reason he's awfully cynical about boxing. Years after the first Sugar Ray Leonard-Roberto Duran fight, I had a chance to see it again on television. You know what? Leonard *didn't* lose that fight on purpose. He fought his heart out. I think he abandoned his usual dancing, stick-and-run style of fighting because he wanted some respect; he wanted to show the world that he could stand still, trade punches with Duran, and still come out on top.

When I was a kid, I turned Duran's victory in that fight into an excuse to become jaded. I grabbed on to a cynical explanation for what had happened and wound up missing something pretty great. I missed that Leonard lost because he did something not many people have the courage to do—he pushed himself beyond his abilities, and so his failure was a noble one. Leonard was willing to risk his perfect boxing record for the chance to see what he was really capable of.

That's not a reason to become cynical. That's a reason to have faith.

CHAPTER THIRTEEN

VULGARITY

Almost twenty years ago, I saw this movie called *Nothing in Common*. Not a great flick, but Tom Hanks is in it, so it's watchable. Tom plays an advertising agency guy who's won a big airline account. Just as he's about to travel to a big meeting with the airline's top executives, his pain-in-the-neck father gets hospitalized and needs to have surgery. Tom—being a good guy—decides he's going to stay and care for his dad, and let someone else take his place at the meeting.

He tells the head of the airline (a man who's as pushy as his father) what he's doing, but the airline guy won't accept it. Tom doesn't budge; he needs to be with his dad. Exasperated, the airline guy tells Tom he's going to count to five, and by the time he's done counting, Tom better have changed his mind. He starts pushing Tom while he's counting. "One, two . . ."

Tom explodes. Mild-mannered Tom Hanks, who hasn't so much as raised his voice for the first hour-and-a-half of the movie. "Three, four, five!" he thunders back in the guy's face. "And don't you *ever* f_____ing touch me again!"

The audience I saw the movie with gasped at that exchange. I mean, I've seen entire horror movies that didn't get as much reaction from a crowd as that one sentence from Tom Hanks. We sat there in the dark, shocked.

When was the last time you were shocked by the f-word? Or by any cursing? Watch HBO or any other pay cable channel, and it feels like cursing is all you hear. It's used casually, and as every part of speech. It's an adjective: *Let's go to the f-ing store*. It's a verb: *She f-ed up her hair!* It's even a noun: *You're such a dumb f-*. Sometimes it's every part of speech in the same sentence: *F- you, you f-ing f-*.

And that's a shame. Cursing used to mean something.

I learned how to curse on the playground at Lanai Road School in Encino, California. I was eight years old. The third grade was lined up to go back to class after recess, and while we waited, this kid named Jason told me to say "bull," and I did. Then he told me to say the s-word, which I'd never even heard before. I shrugged and did that, too. "Now," he said, all solemn, "say them both together." I did, and he gasped. "Go say it to Dede Katz," he said, but by then I got it: this cursing was powerful stuff. "No way," I said. He dared me, I dared him back, and we each decided that the other was a chicken, because neither of us would say "bull__" in front of Dede.

A few weeks later, he taught me a new word, one he'd

heard his brother use. It started with the letter f. When I say Jason taught me the word, I mean he spelled it for me, he told me that it rhymed with "truck," but *he would not actually say it.* "That's the worst word in the whole world," he told me as we hung by our arms from the jungle gym. "They'll kick you out of school for saying it." Here was Jason, who'd been in the principal's office for slugging two different boys in our class and for talking back to Miss Voyne, and he was afraid to say a one-syllable word out loud.

A few years and three thousand miles later, I tried out the f-word for the first time on a playground in Connecticut, where my family had just moved. Tony Verrico and I were playing one-on-one basketball, and he fouled me pretty hard. The word kind of came out of me, and it startled him. He immediately apologized for what he'd done—clearly, if I was saying the f-word, things had gotten serious—and then he walked off the court. That was the power of cursing: it was strong enough to make people take notice, and at the same time it was unpleasant enough to make them turn away.

Cursing had a real place when I was a kid. It was a way of expressing extreme anger or fear. Since we didn't curse that much, when we did, it had a real effect. Swearing at someone could start a fight; swearing after someone hit you could end that fight. Basically, swearing meant you weren't kidding around.

Now it doesn't seem to mean much of anything. Swearing has become just another lazy way of communicating, like saying "you know" or "I mean." It's filling to make sentences longer. (If you were old enough to watch modern gangster movies like *Scarface*, I'd suggest a little experiment. I'd tell you to write down any six or seven sentences of dialogue, cross out the cursing, and watch it magically shrink to two or three lines of dialogue. But you're *not* old enough, so I'll spare you.)

Whenever anyone complains about all the swearing on television or in the movies, they always get the same response: it's realism. It's the way people talk. And I can't argue, so instead I'll just amend that answer a little. Endless cursing is the way really vulgar, *lazy* people talk.

How did this happen? How did cursing go from a rare, powerful way to express anger or shock to just another way people talk? I blame comedians.

I'm serious. When I was a kid, I heard Steve Martin doing his stand-up routine when someone in the audience yelled something stupid at him. Martin stopped, looked out at the guy, and smiled. "I remember when I had *my* first beer," he said, and the audience roared. Instead of letting some jerk ruin his show, he found a very sharp way to make fun of the guy and in the process shut him up. If I were standing in front of hundreds of people, I could never have thought of such a clever line. Heck, if I were *alone* I could never have thought of such a clever line.

Years later, I went to see Eddie Murphy play an auditorium near my college. Eddie also had a pretty good stand-up act, and I was excited to see him. About ten minutes into the show, someone from the crowd yelled something dumb. Murphy stopped, looked at the guy . . . and you could feel the room, just waiting for a brilliant put-down. Instead, he used a common three-word vulgarity, which I won't repeat. Suffice it to say it's been heard on every schoolyard in America, coming from the mouths of not-very-smart boys.

I was completely bummed. I'd paid good money to see Murphy, and when he got a chance to show how clever he could be on the spur of the moment, he retreated into simple crudeness. *I* could have thought to say what he said . . . and I wasn't pulling in the big bucks doing comedy. The worst part, though, is that the crowd went wild when he swore at that guy. They gasped, and then they roared. Just being vulgar was enough; the crowd didn't care if Eddie Murphy was actually quick on his feet.

Of course, Murphy wasn't the first guy to notice that saying something "shocking" had the same effect as saying something clever. But he was so popular that he spawned dozens of new comedians who managed to copy his vulgarity, even if they didn't have his genuine talent. In my lifetime, stand-up comedy has gone from guys like Bill Cosby and Bob Newhart, who never had to swear to get a laugh, to foul-mouthed guys like Andrew Dice Clay and most of the folks you find on cable television, who never have to say anything clever to get a laugh.

And as comedians' mouths got nastier and nastier, so

did the mouths of boys everywhere. That's because repeating comedy bits and lines from funny movies is one of the top social skills a boy can have. It's always been that way. My brother knew every routine from Bill Cosby's first couple of albums, I could recite most of *Animal House* word for word, and my friend's kid has *Old School* and *There's Something About Mary* down pat. Repeating funny lines back and forth is how boys find common ground; my college roommates and I *still* begin phone conversations with lines from Bill Murray or Michael Keaton movies.

Boys have an excuse for being vulgar: we aren't very original, and the stuff we choose to repeat has gotten pretty potty-mouthed, so we have, too.

What I can't understand is, why have you girls? Don't tell me I'm wrong; I've stood in too many movie lines and shopping malls, and listened to packs of teenage girls swearing so much they'd make prison inmates blush. (I once heard a mother ask a bunch of foul-mouthed girls at a McDonald's, "Is this why I fought for equal rights? So you can curse like truck drivers?")

Maybe that mom was on to something. Maybe some girls curse so much because they want to prove that they can be like boys in every way. Could be that they mistake swearing for a good way to show self-confidence, because that's what they see cocky guys do. But what they—what *all* girls—need to understand is that certain ways of acting don't travel well between the genders. Even when they're doing the same things, boys and girls are judged differently.

Think about it: if a boy were to hold his friends' hands, giggle a lot, gossip, and obsess about his clothes, he'd be labeled a sissy pretty quick. But you and your friends can do all of that stuff, and it's considered harmless, natural behavior. Likewise, when boys curse up a storm, it's kind of considered par for the course. It's expected, and the worst label a foul-mouthed boy can expect is "obnoxious." If *you* do it, though, if you curse up a blue streak, you run the risk of being thought of as a tramp. For the record, this is a breathtaking double standard—just one more example of how the world can be unfair to girls—but it is how it is; girls who curse a lot are thought of as cheap, and even a little slutty. Ever notice in the movies that the girls with the worst mouths are usually also in the tightest, skimpiest clothes?

❂f course, if you *want* to sound cheap and slutty, because you're tired of having a good reputation, curse all you want. It's a time-tested way to ruin your image.

A few years ago, a teenage actress on a hit show decided she was tired of her character, even though she'd signed a contract that had her locked into the show for another two years. What did she do? She gave an interview to a men's magazine, and proved she's nothing like the girl she plays on television. The magazine asked her what would happen if she ever met the character she played in real life: "I'd

145

kick Mary's f__ing ass," she said. (Though she didn't use abbreviations. I trust you can figure out the words she *did* use.) "I'd kick the s__ out of her."

Nice talk from the girl who played the elder daughter of a minister on *Seventh Heaven,* right? I think maybe Jessica Biel figured her salty talk might upset the show's producers so much they'd fire her. If not, maybe the nearly-naked pictures of her that were also in the magazine would do the trick. In public relations, they call that an image makeover: Jessica Biel must have hoped to make people see her as something other than a Goody Two-shoes.

But if she wanted a new image, why did she have to pick "classless tramp"? The odd thing was that in the same interview, Jessica complained about the fact that she wasn't being considered for good roles in big, mainstream movies. What was odd about that was that it didn't seem to occur to her that the young women who *were* getting the big movies weren't cursing up a storm or showing their breasts in magazines. The women getting the best roles knew what I think Jessica didn't: being vulgar is how you get people's attention if you've got nothing else going for you.*

Here's how a French philosopher made the same point hundreds of years ago: "The last act of a desperate artist is to expose his genitals." I think about that line every time I walk by a newsstand and see some actress who hasn't worked in a while looking out at me from the cover of *Playboy.* When they have nothing more to give, creatively, too many people are happy to settle for being "outrageous" . . . whether it's by taking off their clothes for a girlie magazine or using an endless stream of nasty language. (Or, in Jessica Biel's case, doing both at the same time.)

Two decades ago, it was possible to get an entire theatre to gasp at one, heartfelt curse word. Today, it's hard to get noticed even when you're using a slew of them. Today, the only real power vulgarity has left is to make the person using it sound . . . vulgar.

---

*As of this writing, Jessica Biel *still* hasn't gotten any good roles in mainstream movies, unless you count the lead role in a remake of a 1970s slasher film, *The Texas Chainsaw Massacre*. I sure don't.

CHAPTER FOURTEEN

FAITH

We used to call Rick and Susan the God Squad. We'd watch them pull up in their ancient Volkswagen from the windows of biology class; tall, aw-shucks Rick loping toward the Darien High cafeteria hand in hand with his preppy, beautiful wife. We made fun of their car, we made fun of their corny, unshakeable cheer, but we secretly looked forward to seeing them.

Rick and Susan were part of a Christian ministry, and they held weekly meetings at the homes of different kids. Somehow they'd become a fixture in our school at lunchtime, and somehow they knew every student's name. (A pretty neat trick, considering there were twelve-hundred of us at DHS.) Rick and Susan may have seemed too cheerful to be true, but they managed to spread that cheer. They made us feel good.

I fell in with the God Squadders for the world's most predictable reason: cute girls could be found at Rick and Susan's cafeteria table. Cute girls who immediately took an interest in me because they thought I was taking an interest in Rick and Susan. One of them asked if I'd come to a meeting. (*Alleluia!*) Another told me she'd love it if I gave her a ride. (*Amen!*) I said yes. This talking-to-girls stuff suddenly seemed easy.

It got even easier at my first meeting. Rick and Susan asked me a bunch of questions about the church I was raised in, and when I answered, Susan smiled as if I were the most fascinating boy on the planet. By the time we got to the singing part of the evening—the worst part for most teenage guys—I didn't even really mind. I went home feeling like these were people I could hang with.

So I did. For about three weeks. I was there at the God Squad lunch table; I was there for weekly meetings. I even started to like the singing. Most of all, I liked belonging.

And then I screwed it all up by asking a question. My question came at the end of one of Rick's "talks," which in the church I went to every Sunday, we called sermons. I'd noticed Rick spoke a lot about the path to heaven, and how it could only truly be followed by those who believed exactly what Rick believed, in exactly the way he believed it. At the end of that path was eternal salvation. At the end of that path was heaven. All other paths, Rick told us, led . . . elsewhere.

I asked where. In front of the other kids, I asked Rick what he thought would happen to people who didn't believe in Jesus in just the way that Rick did. (I thought it was a fair question, considering the fact that even most folks I'd known who called themselves Christians didn't believe in many of the things Rick believed.) Rick paused, then said, "That's not for me to say. God will judge them."

Have you ever heard alarm bells in your head? Mine started ringing. Loud. "What about Jews, and Hindus?" I asked. "What about the people who don't believe in Jesus at all? Even if they've been good people, God won't have them in heaven?" Rick's ever-present smile faded, a bit. So did Susan's. "We're all given a choice," Rick said. "When we are given the Good News, we are given the choice. If we embrace Jesus, he embraces us. If not . . ."

Rick let his sentence trail off, just like mob guys do on television. ("You can pay me my money, or Charlie Knuckles here can . . .") When the meeting ended, he told me to stay. Sternly. I said I couldn't, as I had to drive some kids home, and I took off. The fact that neither he nor Susan was smiling at me anymore was creeping me out.

I got some more nasty looks from my fellow God Squadders at school the next day, and from Rick and Susan next time they showed up at the cafeteria. I was no longer welcome at their table. To put it in biblical terms, I was cast out.

You'd think my run-in with the God Squad would have put me off religion, but the weird thing is that it made me pay a lot more attention to the church I was raised in. I had always gone to mass every Sunday; now I started listening. I knew I didn't believe what Rick was preaching—the idea that heaven is an *extremely* exclusive club—but suddenly it became important to figure out what I *did* believe. Did I have faith of my own?

If I did, I sure couldn't find it. The words in the prayers we said as a congregation suddenly seemed like just that to me—words—and they came out of my mouth like lines I had to remember for a school play. I'd spent years memorizing the prayers, but no time thinking about what they meant. I might as well have been reciting cookie recipes. ("And yea, though verily I add the chocolate chips, stirring unto the butter . . .")

My lack of belief in the words started making me look suspiciously at every part of church, especially the people who stood in the pews with me. How was it they could shake my hand and offer me the "sign of peace" and then ten minutes later honk at me in the parking lot if I took too much time backing out of my space? Pretty soon I was convinced that churchgoers were phonies and church was nonsense.

So as soon as I got to college (and out from under my parents' watchful eye) I stopped going to church at all. Oddly enough, though, the question didn't leave my head: did I have faith? Even if all this church stuff really was a farce, I still felt a strong need to sort out my own beliefs about God. Luckily for me, I'd chosen a college with a fine religion department. I figured, why not seek answers *and* earn college credits? I registered for a class about the Bible's New Testament.

Have I mentioned that I'm not always the brightest guy? The courses at Northwestern University had levels assigned: A, B, C, and D. The religion class was a C-level, so I guessed that since C meant average on a report card, it would be pretty easy. Turns out A-levels were the intro courses. I found myself in a class made up mostly of seniors and graduate students, all of whom had taken the introductory courses required by Dr. Perry, the professor. Sometime during the first hour, however, I must have asked a decent question or two, because he ended up waiving the requirement and letting me stay. I think it was a combination of pity and a desire to help his other students by lowering the grade point average.

By about the fourth or fifth session, I understood most of what was being said, and I managed to jump into the conversation. I loved that class. Until halfway through the semester, when a student named Randy casually mentioned something about Mary's other children. Those alarm bells went off in my head, again. Turns out I wasn't good at hiding my shock that some people believed the Virgin Mary went on to have more kids. Dr. Perry asked me to stay after class. "You seem upset," he said.

No kidding. How could anyone who calls himself a Christian say what Randy said? How could the Blessed Virgin have other children? Dr. Perry answered, and his answer changed my life:

"No two people read the Bible exactly the same way," he

said. "And the Gospels themselves don't always agree on everything. But you know what never changes, from book to book, from faith to faith? The message. Whether you're a Christian, a Jew, a Hindu, or a Muslim, you believe that God wants you to do good deeds, and to put other people first. God wants you to pursue goodness and to reject evil."

Now, being a little thick, I kept protesting. "But the whole idea of the Virgin Mary is so important to the story of Jesus."

He agreed but said, "I want you to do something for me. I want you to think about which of Jesus' teachings would be changed if Mary had gone on and had children with Joseph. What lessons would be lost? Then let's talk some more."

Over the months that followed, long past the end of Dr. Perry's class, we did talk some more. We talked about how religions are made up of two things: the stories and the message. The stories are the historical part, the "who, what, where, and when" stuff. The message is the "why." We argue so much about the stories, Dr. Perry taught me, that we fail to see all the common ground in the messages of the major religions.

Once I realized that it was more important for Randy and me to agree on what we believed God wants from us than on whether or not Mary had other children, once I could concentrate on what Jesus taught, I found my faith. It had been there the whole time. Faith wasn't housed in the part of my brain that had memorized prayers; it was in the part of my soul that led me to take Dr. Perry's class, the part that knew something was missing when I stopped going to church.

Just as important, I found my path. Rick and the God Squadders had been right about that; faith *is* a path. What Rick had wrong, I think, is that it's not a direct path, and it's not meant for large groups to walk on. In fact, it's exactly wide enough for one.

My path began in the church my folks attend. That was my foundation. Maybe I didn't accept everything I learned there, but going to their church gave me a starting point. It showed me what faith looked like. When Rick and Susan came along and told me about a different way to believe in God, I was able to compare it to what I'd learned already. I was able to see where the God Squadders' narrow idea of salvation didn't make sense to me. A little further on down the path, I found Dr. Perry, and I learned some more. My path changed a bit.

Here's the important thing: *I stayed on that path.* It took me to some interesting places in college. I signed up for more religion courses. I found ministers and students and, in a synagogue not far from campus, a very patient rabbi to pepper with questions. While visiting the Bahà'ì Temple in the next town, I accidentally locked the keys in my car, only to be rescued by a temple worker who easily unlocked it with a coat hanger. ("I wasn't *always* one of the faithful," he said, smiling.) Once in a while, I even wandered into my old church.

Strangely enough, I learned a lot from atheists, people whose only religious belief is that God doesn't exist. Look at all the suffering in the world, they'd say. How could a Creator allow that? Look at all the violent men in history who used "God's will" as an excuse to do terrible things. Religion, they told me, was invented by corrupt rulers to keep the common folk in line. That said, my friends the atheists would shut their mouths, as if the subject was closed.

I figured out pretty quickly that their mouths weren't the only things they'd shut. Their hearts and minds seemed pretty blocked off, too. They were content to pose big, important questions, but I didn't see them making any real effort to look for answers. And that, I realized, is the best explanation of this path I've been telling you about: it's a search for answers, for meaning, and for an understanding of what God wants from us.

There *are* answers, if you're willing to open your heart and mind enough to try to find them. The trick is to forget about logic, because faith is a belief in things that can't be proved logically. Faith doesn't reside in your cranium, next to history and algebra. Faith is the stuff your gut tells you.

How do I know God exists? Simple: I feel God's presence. When I hear Gospel music, I feel it. When I think of a woman I met in Chicago, who happily cooks hot meals for her poor, elderly neighbors most nights even though she can barely afford her own grocery bills, I feel it. When I watch my daughter stand up for a friend, even though it will put her at odds with the "popular" girls, I feel it. When a shortstop makes an impossibly graceful, diving catch, and when Prince plays the guitar part at the end of "Purple Rain," I feel it. Goodness and beauty aren't things that could appear in a god-less world, as far as I'm concerned. They are reasons to believe, reasons to have faith.

Aside from that, I won't use this space to tell you what I've learned about God. You've got to find your own answers. Start in a church or a synagogue or a mosque. Listen a lot. Ask questions. Make sure that whatever religious community you join appreciates your value as a woman. (I left my folks' church partly because it *still* won't let women play any leadership role, centuries after it was founded. Some folks are taking longer to climb out of the Stone Age than others, I guess.)

Most of all, seek inspiration. Though some people claim that God calls to them when they're alone, I think for most of us God is found in the actions and words of others. Sometimes we feel close to our maker when we're sitting in a pew, listening to a guy in a robe, and sometimes we're moved by the Godliness we see when we're helped by a total stranger. You sort of have to be on the lookout, because you never really know when God will make an appearance.

A friend told me this story:

A man named Ted wakes up, turns on the television, and hears the weatherman say that so much rain is coming it might flood his town. Sure enough, it starts pouring. Ted's next-door neighbor comes by and says, "I've got room in my car, and I think maybe we'd better get out of here before it gets any worse." Ted thanks him, but declines, saying, "God will look after me."

That afternoon, the nearby river has risen so much that Ted's house has a foot of water in it. A local policeman in hip boots comes by and says, "Sir, I think you should come with me before this gets any worse. I'll take you to higher ground." Ted declines again, saying, "God will protect me."

By nightfall, Ted's house is almost completely underwater. He sits on the roof, with an umbrella, and sees a rescue helicopter pulling neighbors off their roofs. When the copter comes to his house, he waves it away shouting, "Don't worry about me. God will save me."

An hour later, the local dam breaks, Ted is swept off his roof, and he drowns. He finds himself standing at the Pearly Gates, soaking wet, in the presence of the Lord. Angrily, he says, "I believed in you! Why didn't you rescue me?"

"What are you talking about?" God says. "I tried three times!"

Unlike a lot of the gooey, "inspirational" stuff that gets passed around in e-mails, I really like that story, because it gets at the most wonderful thing about faith: to find God, you don't have to cast your glance upwards, you merely have to look around you. Proof of God's existence—and bottomless love—is easy to find, if you make the effort to look for it. You'll find that proof in the words of a preacher, in the actions of a nurse, and in the work of an artist. When you choose to step onto your own path of faith, you'll catch glimpses of God everywhere you look.

Including the mirror.

CHAPTER FIFTEEN

HOW TO BE HAPPY

Imagine you're reading a really good book of short stories, only to find that the last few pages of each tale are missing. Now imagine discovering that book's missing pages two decades later, and finally learning what happened to each of those characters you'd almost forgotten.

That's pretty much what going to your twentieth high school reunion is like.

I went to mine a few years ago, and I came away from it having learned three very useful lessons. First, high school jock + twenty years of drinking beer on the couch = not very pretty picture. Second, while it's incredibly shallow to show off one's beautiful wife at one's high school reunion—making sure to introduce her to all the girls who turned me (oops, I mean turned "one") down for dates—it's also *really* satisfying. The third thing I learned is that happiness does not always find the people you think it will. In fact, happiness is completely unpredictable.

Standing among people I had known pretty well twenty

years earlier, I was kind of shocked to notice that the folks who seemed to "have it all" didn't necessarily seem any happier than the people who you or I might think of as failures. Happiness was something people found (or didn't) regardless of all the stuff that's supposed to *bring* it: the guys who drove to the reunion in Porsches were no more likely to be happy than the guys in ten-year-old mini-vans.

How can that be, when everything we see on television tells us that happiness comes from being the best or having the most? I wondered about that a lot, and then I looked up the word in my trusty dictionary: "A feeling of pleasure, contentment, or joy." No mention of achievement. Not one word about owning stuff. That might explain why Scott, a kid I used to ride my bike with, seemed so unhappy even though he now owns a pretty large company and lives in a house roughly the size of Rhode Island. His workday is a grind, he told me: he's always worried about staying on top of things. When I asked him if he still goes to the movies like we did in high school, he looked at me as if I'd just landed from Mars and said, "Who has time?"

Scott has achieved pretty much everything he set out to, and it doesn't make him happy. P.J., on the other hand, never got any farther than the next town and lives in a house about half the size of the one he grew up in. He has three handsome little boys ("They're easy on the eyes, but tough on the furniture," his wife told me, laughing), and though he works his tail off and still doesn't make enough money to take his family on fancy vacations, he may be the happiest guy to come out of Darien High, class of '81. I asked him what his secret is. I asked him why he seems so happy. He shrugged. "It beats being unhappy," he said.

I had always thought of happiness as something we achieve, a goal we set for ourselves. If I can just get that A+, I'll be happy. When I can afford that watch/car/house, I'll be happy. If that woman falls for me, I'll be happy. Like most people, I thought happiness comes from getting the things you want.

But none of those things ever worked for me, at least not for long. I talked my dad into letting me buy a little red Audi before my senior year of college, and while it was fun to show off for a week, it didn't make me "happy" in any lasting way. I got my own column in the college paper, and people would stop me on the street to talk about stuff I'd written, but being noticed brought only brief moments of satisfaction. No one thing ever seemed to drive away the doubts, disappointments, slights, and insecurities that made me generally *un*happy.

And then—lo and behold—years after college I realized I had *become* happy. How that had happened remained a mystery to me until I spoke with P.J. at the reunion. I was happy because it beat being unhappy. Let me put it another way:

My brother Leo is a really talented photographer. He's taken pictures of waterfalls in Yosemite National Park and cityscapes in Northern California. He's gotten remarkable shots of Alcatraz Island rising from the fog in the San Francisco Bay. He uses film, not digital, and he develops and prints his own stuff. To do that, he needs total darkness. Now, does Leo *wait* for total darkness so he can do his work? Does he hope for a cloudy, moonless night, and a power outage that will knock out streetlights? Of course not: he's built himself a dark room. He finds the dark conditions he needs by dealing with all possible sources of light. He closes himself in a space that has no windows, an electric light he can turn off, and coverings that block light from coming in under the door or around any of its edges.

While happiness isn't as easy to create as darkness is, the way you get there isn't much different: if you want to be happy, you have to start by dealing with the different things that can make you miserable.

What causes you stress? Is it schoolwork, or all the after-school commitments you have? Maybe it's the social stuff going on around you, and maybe there are even bigger, personal things you're dealing with. Just maybe it's all of the above, and then some. If that's the case, you've read this chapter so far and thought, "Is he crazy? How can I be happy when I'm dealing with so much?" I understand. Life can feel overwhelming, which is why trying to manage all the stuff that stresses you out is the first step toward finding happiness.

First things first: **get yourself organized**. Make sure

your schoolwork is kept in one place. Clean out your back-pack, as well as your desk or wherever it is that you study. Create a routine for dealing with your homework, whether you have a checklist or a way of putting papers back into your notebook as you finish them. Keep a calendar, so you can see things like athletic meets, music lessons, and big school projects coming, and so you can be ready for them.

See, if you're organized when you do your schoolwork, you can tell right away when a particular subject is causing you problems—for instance, that it's taking you three times as long to do your math homework as your history —and you can deal with it. A student who shows a teacher an organized notebook when she comes in to ask for extra help is going to get a much better reaction than the kid who has to dig through a hundred crumpled papers to find her notes.

If you keep a calendar, you can see when you're not giv-ing yourself enough time to do things well . . . and maybe more important, you can prove to your folks or your teach-ers that you need a little help lightening the load. What happens when you get yourself organized is that you be-come more self-confident . . . you find you're running your life, and your life isn't running you. Though the happiest people I've met are pretty different from each other, one thing they all have in common is self-confidence.

Once you're organized and feeling pretty in control of the stuff that you do, take a good look at the kids you choose to be around. Do the people you hang out with make you feel good . . . and happy? Or is there so much pressure to be seen with the right crowd and at the right parties that you're anxious a lot? Do your friends support you, or expect you to toe the line and do what *they* think is cool? **Figure out who your *real* friends are.** Be honest with yourself about this stuff, because your friends are maybe the biggest influences in your life . . . and so making sure you're surrounded by people who are going to lift you up (and not tear you down) is incredibly important.

While we're talking about friends, a quick thought about popularity. Most kids who qualify as "popular" are hardly "well-liked and well-respected," which is how the dictionary defines the word. Nope, they tend to be the most feared and envied kids . . . and while it might sound nice to be envied—it certainly helps your social life for awhile—it's not something people will remember you fondly for years later.

Like at your twentieth high school reunion. You know what was really interesting about mine? The most popular kids turned out to be the *least* likely to be happy. While a few of them had moved past the idea that social standing is the most important thing in the world, a bunch spent college and their working lives trying to recapture their status as the Queens and Kings of the cafeteria. (There are a dozen great songs about this sad little phenomenon, like Guster's "Homecoming King" and Bruce Springsteen's "Glory Days.") For as much as you might envy the kids who lord their popularity over you in school today, chances are pretty good you'll pity them somewhere down the road.

Which leads me to the next step on that road to happiness: **count on karma.** Buddhists believe in reincarnation—the notion that we come back to this world over and over. They think that the quality of our current life is decided by our behavior in our past lives. (In other words, the rat you see in the gutter might be reincarnated from a schoolyard bully.) They call this belief karma. Now, I don't know about past lives, but I have total faith in what John Lennon called "Instant Karma." I believe that the energy you put out into the world—your karma—comes back to you pretty quickly. That's not a flaky or mystical belief, like astrology. Karma, in the "what goes around, comes around" sense of the word, is really just common sense: if you're kind to people, they'll be there for you when you need them, and if you're not . . . well, let's just say your failures will have a cheering section.

When I was in eighth grade and about as insecure as it's possible to be, the most popular guy in school suddenly decided to be my friend. I was in heaven: we walked through the halls of Middlesex Junior High doing *Saturday Night Live* skits, and I found myself invited to the same parties he went to. The girls who liked him—the prettiest girls from both junior high schools in Darien—were suddenly calling me, hoping I'd put in a good word for them. For about a month, I basked in the reflected glow of the sun.

167

And then the sun set. On me. At a party at our friend Lisa's house, Mr. Popular talked me into doing my lip-synced impression of this singer named Boz Scaggs for a bunch of people. He dimmed the lights, put the song on the stereo, and introduced me: "Ladies and gentlemen: Phil Van *Scaaaaaggs*." A minute into it, I realized I was being laughed at . . . and the guy laughing the hardest was the guy who had pushed me to perform for everybody. I stopped, and I found myself glad that the lights were low, so no one could see the color of my face. My "friend" asked why I had stopped, and when I told him I didn't much appreciate being laughed at, he announced—in front of all the kids—that that was a shame, because being laughed at was what I did best.

He didn't stop there. He went on to do an impression of his own: me, trying to do chin-ups in gym. Everybody laughed some more. Then he did me, stammering as I tried to talk to girls. The audience was rolling. I don't remember how I got out of Lisa's family room that night, but I remember hiding in the woods outside her house, wondering how I could ever show my face again.

I *hated* him. For weeks, I wondered what I could do to get back at him, how I could get even. Though there wasn't much I could do—he was much more popular and a lot stronger than I was—that didn't stop me from spending hours planning revenge. In a way, he had more power over my life than ever, because I believed that the only way I'd ever feel good about myself was if I got back at him . . . if I made him feel as lousy as I did. What I didn't understand was that *I* was the one making myself feel lousy; he'd moved on to his next victim and wasn't giving me any thought.

Not long after, the guy left for another school . . . and then the strangest thing happened: people started trashing him. He was a jerk, they'd say. Even the most popular girls were suddenly referring to him as a conceited pretty boy. It turns out I didn't need to do anything to make him look bad, because people didn't like him to begin with. They had laughed at me that night for pretty much the same reason I had performed for them: we all wanted to please Mr. Popular. We had *all* given him too much power over our lives . . . and now that we no longer feared him, our collective bad feelings for him sort of exploded out of us. When I noticed that he was never again invited to my classmates' parties, even when he was home on break, I almost felt sorry for him. Almost.

When people hurt your feelings, count on "karma" to eventually make everything right, and move on. The cruelty they've shown you will come back to them. It may take awhile, and you may not be around to see it, but it *will* happen. Once you really understand that, you'll be able to let those people—and the power they have over you—go, and you'll spend a lot less time with the horrible feelings and thoughts that make happiness so hard.

You know, while you're in there, clearing your head (and heart) of bad feelings, do a quick check for the ones you bring on yourself. Think about the stuff you do that seems like fun while you're doing it, but leaves you feeling a little lousy. Then make an effort to stop doing it; try to **filter out the poison.** For me, that poison comes in all kinds of forms, including those shows that celebrate other people's wealth. ("Hey, it's another fabulous home that *you'll* never have! And here's a half-million dollar sports car!") I used to be hooked on one in particular, called *Lifestyles of the Rich and Famous*. Being neither, I felt like a failure every time I watched the British host with a silly voice raise his glass of champagne aboard some yacht on the French Riviera. Once I stopped watching, I felt better.

Gossip is a major form of poison that makes the people who do it feel unhappy, eventually. It's fun to dish the dirt or to know a secret about somebody else, but the problem is that the stuff passed around is almost always negative. Gossip is meant to tear someone else down—not great for one's karma, you know?—but all it really does is make the person spreading it look bad.

And feel bad. The urge to gossip comes from our own insecurities. We think that if we trash someone else, people won't look too closely at *us*. It doesn't work. Picture the people you know that gossip the most. What do you really think of those people? Aren't you a little guarded around them, afraid that they'll turn on you? Is that how *you* want to be thought of? I know how hard it is to avoid gossip—I still fail at it pretty regularly—but what isn't so hard is to tone it down. To make a decision not to take part in really hurtful stuff, and to shut down the people who spread it. There's nothing like a quick "I feel funny talking about her behind her back" to stop gossip in its tracks, and to serve warning on the person spreading it that you're a bigger, more secure person than they are.

This is all hard work. Getting organized, choosing friends wisely, trusting karma to handle the people who've hurt you, and filtering out the bad feelings you bring on yourself each require a lot of effort. Here's something that will make all of these things easier: **open your mind**. Accept that you don't know everything, and that some of the things you *do* think you know are wrong. That's one of those abilities we lose pretty early in life, and it's a shame, because someone who can keep an open mind can accomplish a lot more, and be loads happier, than someone who believes that opinions are supposed to be carved in stone and defended unto death. (Which would describe me, from age twelve to . . . well, to more recently than I care to admit. Trust me when I say I spent a long, long time being a close-minded bonehead.)

When you're a little kid, you change your mind about stuff all the time, and it doesn't bother you. Maybe you think the stove looks like a cool thing to climb on, and then one day you get up there, and your hand gets a little crispy when you find one of the burners is still hot . . . so

171

you decide you were wrong about that stove. That's called *learning*. You don't know something, you learn, and you change the way you think.

Somewhere along the line, though, it starts to feel embarrassing to admit that you don't know something—or are wrong about something—so you become stubborn. You dig in when you should let go. Suddenly, 98 percent of the fights you have with your friends happen because one or both of you are too stubborn to own up to being wrong. Usually about something trivial. The good news is that by being open-minded and admitting your error when you find out *you're* the one who's wrong, you can avoid half of those fights.

And you can make even better friends. Most of us gravitate toward people who are open-minded and honest. Folks whose minds are flexible are easier to talk to, they don't make the people around them feel so defensive, and basically, they just seem happier. That's because it takes a secure person to be open-minded. It takes a self-confident person. As I said a few pages ago, self-confidence is really important if you aim to be happy.

So is spreading the wealth. **Be the cause of happiness in others.** I don't mean that you have to always do what other people want or spend your life catering to the whims of your family and friends. I mean that you should make a real effort to be kind to the folks around you. Be polite. When people do things for you, however small, thank them sincerely. When you spot an opportunity to help, grab it. Maybe you see a woman with a baby stroller up the street, struggling to open a shop door. Run ahead and do it for her. Smile when you hold the door. That won't be hard, because doing small kindnesses tend to make you feel great. Do things for people with no expectation that they'll ever be able to return the favor. (This is *wonderful* for your karma.) To be happy, spread happiness.

The best way to do that is to try to be the friend *you'd* most like to have. Listen—really listen—to the people in your life. Look them in the eye when they speak. So often we just want to feel like someone is hearing us. Be that person for others. Be that true friend.

And for yourself, be the very best friend in the world. **Take care of your *whole* self.** When we talked about beauty, I mentioned that you need to get a good balance in your diet to be healthy and strong. Well, happiness works the same way. To be happy, you need to make sure you're feeding your mind, your body, and your spirit.

Your mind craves knowledge, and while you're getting plenty of that in school, it's not enough. Make sure you're aware of the world around you. Read a newspaper; listen to people discuss politics. Pick up books that aren't assigned, but seem interesting. (If it turns out that they're not interesting, put them down. Life's too short to read boring books.) Figure out what interests you, and learn all you can about it. Use that free time you now have because you've gotten your schoolwork so organized.

Take care of your body through diet and exercise.

There's a reason people wish each other health and happiness: those things mostly go hand-in-hand. Doctors have done a million studies proving the effects of physical health on mental health. Did you know that when you exercise, your body produces chemicals that make you happy? But even if the body didn't, it's just common sense that it's hard to feel good when you don't feel *well*.

Finally, dearest daughter, feed your spirit. Look at the world around you and see the beauty in it. Be inspired by that beauty to create some of your own. Paint, dance, take pictures, write . . . it doesn't really matter what you do—or how well you do it—as long as you're expressing the things you think and feel in some artistic way. Try not to dwell on your differences with people, but instead find comfort in your remarkable similarities. Practice kindness. Search for God, and when you find Her, thank Her for Her many blessings.

On a warm weekend night a few summers ago, I found myself surrounded by people I hadn't been with in twenty years. When I had last seen them at the end of high school, I'd probably already finished growing physically. But I'd only just begun growing as a person. Standing in that restaurant, I found myself almost overwhelmed with happiness. Not just because I could tell my old classmates about the wonderful person I had married, or the two lovely, loving daughters I was raising. I felt happy for those reasons, to be sure, but also because for the first time in a very long time, I remembered the skinny, insecure kid who had left Darien High all those years ago . . . and I saw just how much he'd learned. I saw how far he'd come.

That, dearest daughter, is my greatest wish for you: that you'll look back one day and be shocked by how far *you've* come. For now, keep trying, keep making fabulous mistakes, and keep dreaming. Aim high, and don't worry so much about everyone else's expectations, including your dad's. What's most important in life—what will *really* bring you happiness—is that one day you're able to take a good look at yourself and find you've become the person that *you* always hoped you'd be.

ABOUT THE AUTHOR

Philip Van Munching is the author of two previous books. His political and social commentary has appeared on the Op-Ed pages of *The New York Times* and the *Chicago Tribune*. He also writes the "Devil's Adman" column for *Brandweek*. He and his wife, Christina, live with their daughters in New York City.